A Private Sphere

Digital Media and Society

A Private Sphere

Democracy in a Digital Age

ZIZI A. PAPACHARISSI

polity

First published in 2010 by Polity Press

Polity Press
65 Bridge Street
Cambridge CB2 1UR, UK

Polity Press
350 Main Street
Malden, MA 02148, USA

ISBN-13: 978-0-7456-4524-7
ISBN-13: 978-0-7456-4525-4 (pb)

A catalogue record for this book is available from the British Library.

Typeset in 9.5 on 12.5 pt FF Scala
by Servis Filmsetting Ltd, Stockport, Cheshire
Printed and bound in Great Britain by MPG Books Group Limited, Bodmin, Cornwall

The publisher has used its best endeavours to ensure that the URLs for external websites referred to in this book are correct and active at the time of going to press. However, the publisher has no responsibility for the websites and can make no guarantee that a site will remain live or that the content is or will remain appropriate.

Every effort has been made to trace all copyright holders, but if any have been inadvertently overlooked the publisher will be pleased to include any necessary credits in any subsequent reprint or edition.

For further information on Polity, visit our website: www.politybooks.com

Contents

Acknowledgements

To parents, academic and non

I wrote this book to offer an alternative explanation for how people connect to others in contemporary democracies. I owe thanks to all my friends and mentors, academic and non, who indulged me and discussed my ideas with me, agreeing, or challenging my assumptions, or offering their own perspective on what it means to be a citizen now. Above all, I appreciate you being interested. I borrow concepts from a variety of disciplines to piece together the argument for a private sphere, so I am indebted to Chuck Whitney, interdisciplinary guru and mega-mentor, for showing me how to be interdisciplinary without sacrificing argument integrity. I thank Rod Hart, for pushing me to think through the limits of my argument and beyond linguistic conventions used to describe the abstract (in this case, that was: "That's all good Zizi, but what happens to the rest of the world when we are all enclosed in our private spheres?"). Mark Deuze introduced me to Andrea and Polity and encouraged me to continue thinking of *prodused* content as an act of political dissent, and I am grateful for that. And I am indebted to Andrea Drugan, my wonderful editor at Polity, for her insight and faith in my vision for this book. I also would like to thank Steve Jones and Dwight McBride at the University of Illinois-Chicago, and Concetta Stewart and Betsy Leebron at Temple University for their support and kindness. Huge thanks go to my students for allowing me to ramble on about this stuff in class and being a constant source of inspiration. Finally, a heartfelt thanks to Stella, for advising me to write this like I am telling a story to someone and reminding me to have fun with it.

1

Contemporary Democracies, Civic Engagement, and the Media

"Change life!" "Change society!" These precepts mean nothing without the production of an appropriate space . . . new social relationships call for a new space, and vice versa.

Lefebvre (1974/1991, p. 59)

On the evening of November 4, 2008, the day of the fifty-sixth United States presidential election, thousands of Chicago residents enthusiastically made their way to Grant Park, where the soon-to-be next President of the United States, Barack Obama, would be hosting an election night party. While the entire park area was available to Obama supporters to celebrate, and crowd projections neared a million, a smaller area had been sectioned off for the media and a few thousand attendees who were fortunate enough to procure tickets to the event. Tickets had been made available just a few days earlier, via a complex network of contacts assembled through Obama's Illinois supporters – people who had made donations, worked in phone banks, traveled to battleground states to campaign for Obama, or signed up to receive e-mail updates from the campaign. The Obama campaign had gained a level of media-savvy notoriety by using cell phone data to send context-specific text messages, Facebook applications, and a variety of new media tools in innovative ways during the campaign.

On the night of the election, ticket holders had to proceed through a variety of screening points, so as to be admitted, ticket in hand, to the event. Seven screening points and three security checks later, the last of which employed a screening protocol equivalent to that of boarding a commercial air carrier, ticket holders were admitted to the event, equipped with giant screens, showing the latest results and result projections. The same mega-screens had been placed throughout the remainder of the park and in other public areas. Forced to wait for several hours until the results would be final and the President-elect would appear on the stage, these select few thousands amused themselves by commenting on the variety of a generally festive mix of music played on the PA system and election coverage, courtesy of CNN. Event attendees discontent with the level of information provided by CNN quickly pulled out their mobile devices, mostly iPhones or Blackberries, and googled results and projections as reported by other mainstream media and alternative news sources. Those seeking even higher levels of involvement were actively updating their status on Facebook and tweeting their latest impressions of the event they were attending. Several, if not the majority, of the attendees spent a great deal of time on their cell phones, communicating with others. A popular conversation topic, and close second to election results, was wifi access and cell phone signal availability, or lack thereof. One might expect that media access, essential to experience the event live, from home, would become irrelevant to those select few attending the coveted event live. On the contrary, for those at the event, the absence of convenient domestic access to media was felt, and addressed, through the use of mobile devices.

When eventually, at 10 p.m. Central Time, Barack Obama was proclaimed President-elect, the crowd cheered enthusiastically. It was a historic moment; the first African-American President of the United States to be elected. Everyone was emotional, many cheered, several wept tears of joy, hugged, and waited, in a state of mixed elation and disbelief, for President Obama to appear for his acceptance speech. As the President emerged on the stage, cheers, cries of joy, and music all blended together in jubilant noise; people clapped; and most raised not flags or other emblems of fraternity but their cell phones and cameras, in salute, to the new President-elect. As they took photographs, captured video, or just left the line open for loved ones on the other end listening in, the new President began to address a crowd of digitally enabled and digitally extended citizens (see image 1).

There is this mystical connection between technology and

Figure 1: *On election night, November 2008, Chicago crowds welcome President-elect Obama, mobile devices in hand*

democracy. Not all technologies are democratizing or democracy-related. Most technology has little to do with the condition of democracy. Yet, technologies that afford expressive capabilities, like the radio, television, the Internet, and related media, tend to trigger narratives of emancipation, autonomy, and freedom in the public imagination. All too often then, we wonder, at the appearance of a newer communication medium, how it will affect our conventions of democratic governance. Usually, these discourses are framed within utopian and dystopian polarities that represent hopes and fears projected onto these newer technologies. It is not uncommon for people to make sense of the new by categorizing it as positive or negative, as a way of relating it to their everyday lives and goals.

Democracy naturally combines these personal trajectories of advancement and failure in everyday life through a commonly shared system of decision-making. More than a political system of governance, a democracy is a guarantee of equality, freedom, the possibility of civic virtue or *areté*. To the Ancient Greeks, *areté* extended beyond civic obligations and was used to express the point where an individual attains a state of excellence, approaching the true and optimal essence of what it means to be a human being. *Areté* was the journey to and the outcome of a fulfilled life, a life lived to its fullest potential, and thus a happy life. It is telling that the notion of *areté* is irrevocably connected to the condition of democracy for the Ancient Greeks, and this marks the conception of democracy as an ideal state of governance.

It is perhaps this ideal state that Olafur Eliasson, Danish-Icelandic artist and professor/founder of the Institut für Raumexperimente, a laboratory for spatial research, had in mind as he envisioned a permanent outdoor installation for the Bard College campus entitled *Parliament of reality* (see images 2 and 3). A contemporary play on the *Althing*, the Icelandic Parliament, founded around AD 930 and held outdoors until the late eighteenth century, *Parliament of reality* is a complex art installation meant to create new spaces that evoke and permit the practice of democratic deliberation. This contemporary interpretation of a deliberative space is structured around a circular island in the center of a pond, paved with stones in a pattern echoing the meridian lines of nautical charts and the compass. The island was envisioned as a space where individuals could come together and negotiate ideas and arguments, in other words, a contemporary agora or *public sphere* (www.bard.edu/ccs/exhibitions/sites/permanent.php?g=394130&type=1, accessed February 4, 2010).

Eliasson has created several installations founded upon the overlap of public and private, outdoor and indoor spaces. His work is mostly about how space is modified by perception, and how perception itself is modified by the geometries of space, thus approaching the question of the social construction of space from a variety of different contexts. His *Weather project* (www.olafureliasson.net/works/the_weather_project_5.html, accessed February 4, 2010) simulated the outdoor conditions of weather and the experience of sun in the indoor setting of Tate Modern open space, thus inviting visitors to reconcile and adjust their conventions of outdoor and indoor behavioral reactions to the weather. Other

Figures 2 and 3: Parliament of reality, 2006–2009, *by day and by night. Concrete, stone, stainless steel, water, trees, other plants. Dimensions variable; CCS Bard and The Luma Foundation. Photo: Karl Rabe;* © *2009 Olafur Eliasson.*

works, like the *New York City Waterfalls* (www.nycwaterfalls.org, accessed February 4, 2010), challenge our conventional understandings of space and distance, while his most recent exhibition, *Take your time*, uses spatial reconstructions of geometric shapes and color to engage how visitors perceive themselves in relation to space in everyday life and vice versa (www.moma.org/interactives/ exhibitions/2008/olafureliasson/#/intro/, accessed February 4, 2010).

As a permanent installation, *Parliament of reality* is of interest here because it proposes a new contemporary space for the pursuit of imperatives that have guided our understanding of equality, freedom, and community for millennia. This new space, constructed within an established structure, is intended to inspire a re-interpretation of how we socially relate to space, time, and each other. Individuals are temporarily disconnected from their surroundings and placed within an island of deliberation, so as to reconnect with each other through conversation. The installation functions as comment on the present state of democratic deliberation and suggestion for the reinvention of discourse. Of course, it is unclear whether the artist was intentionally responding to Lefebvre's call for the production of new spaces that sustain new social relationships, only for them to be reinvigorated by the novelty of relationships they help create. Yet, the installation claims place, constructs new space, and invites participants to re-examine how they connect to each other. *Parliament of reality* could have been constructed anywhere on the Bard College campus, yet it is telling that the artist saw fit to place it within a pond, to be connected with the remainder of the campus through a bridge, the shape of which shifts as individuals traverse it to enter the parliament. In disconnecting citizens only to reconnect them again, Eliasson acknowledges the need for temporary retreat from the public spaces that we occupy, re-use, and possibly tire of during our everyday routines to a private new space, connected, but also removed from that which is formally defined as public. The artist plays with our conventional understandings of public and private, as this private space is invented solely for the purpose of inspiring public communication. And it is telling, of course, that the experience of traversing the connective bridge is crafted so as to emphasize the shift in perspective that occurs as the traveler leaves public space and approaches a private realm, constructed solely for the purpose of communication.

Parliament of reality relies on a reorganization of space to suggest the possibilities for new relations and conversations that may occur in the geographies of new space. This book is about the reorganization of space that technology permits, and the social relations and conversation that emerge and inspire it. It is common to connect technology to the discovery or rediscovery of the new. Thus, it is technologies of transportation and communication that enable discoveries of new worlds of expression, activity, and prosperity through narratives of utopian hopes and dystopian fears that make for a *geography of the new* (Morley, 2007). These mostly imagined geographies of the new have been the subject of scholarly attention through a variety of analytical tools. Lewis Mumford (1934) employed the construct of the machine to explicate the interplay between technology and civilizations, via processes that were both socially shaped and shaping of technology. Carey (1989) told the story of the telegraph to explain the ability of technology to reconfigure time and space, thus restructuring conventional geographies and proposing new ones. Similarly, Marvin (1990) traced how the decoupling of time and space enabled by electricity and the telephone reorganized social relations, and more recently Gitelman (2006) compared technologies of sound recording and digital recording to show how media become both subjects and instruments of history making. What is of interest here is the ability of media to transform and be transformed by social relations, via processes that lead to revised and newer social routines, rituals, and communicative habits. This book is about the new(er) and reinvented civic habits that emerge out of democracy's complicated relationship with technology.

Media and the mythology of the new

We have become accustomed to greeting the new, including new technology, via the discursive polarities of utopia and dystopia. The stories that we imagine about technologies reflect corresponding mythologies of our expectations of the new and our disillusionment with the old. Utopia, as Laclau (1991) suggests, becomes "the essence of any communication and social practice" (p. 93). We acknowledge this tendency, but rarely do we question this morally based bias to view things as inherently positive or negative, good or bad, helpful or disadvantageous. To a certain extent, this is part of a natural reaction to organize events surrounding us, and categorize them within our individual ecologies as beneficial or contradictory. These myths of technologically enabled utopias or dystopias then predispose our reaction to technological innovation in ways that operate outside the realm of pragmatism. And yet, the power of the myth lies not in its ability to reflect reality, but rather in the promise it holds for escaping or reinventing it. Mosco (2004) suggests that, "useful as it is to recognize lie in the myth . . . myths mean more than falsehoods . . . they are stories that animate individuals and societies by providing paths to transcendence that lift people out of the banality of everyday life. They offer an entrance to another reality, a reality once characterized by the promise of the sublime" (p. 3). Essential as it is to ground our expectations of technology in reality, it is equally necessary to acknowledge the myths that drive our proclivity to use it. Yet it is in this complex weave of reality and fantasy that technology interacts with culture – thus, in Heidegger's (1954/1977) terms, simultaneously *enframing* and *de-worlding* the ontology of human existence.

Myth does not operate without metaphor. Metaphor permits the comparison of new experiences to past ones. It is employed to capture the meaning of contemporary events and inject elements of continuity into experiences that, without it, appear fragmented and accidental. All too often we use metaphors of the past to understand the new, thus contributing to a mythology of the new that bears little relation to reality. Needless to say, metaphor, as part of mythology, possesses solely explanatory power, and ceases to be effective when employed in a prescriptive manner. In a sense, this book is about metaphors that no longer work, and new language that emerges to describe newer civic habits and reform existing ones. What is new about these habits comes from the ways in which they challenge expectations we hold of democracy and the ways in which democratic conventions adjust to respond to these habits.

Metaphor and subsequent myth function in ways that are simultaneously emancipatory and restrictive. A.H. Gunkel and D.J. Gunkel (1997) have argued that expectations and experience of the past can frequently confine the promise of new technology, determining its future by the words used to refer to it, and thus rendering "naming . . . an exercise in power" (p. 133). Utopian and dystopian narratives permit individuals to incorporate new media into their individual ethical hierarchies, thus exercising power and ascribing ethical identity to technological artifacts that possess no specific ethos. This is a human "gesture" upon the space suggested by newer media, a way for living beings to make their mark, and then remark, space, actual and imaginary (Lefebvre, 1974/1991). Electronic media, in particular, routinely evoke the dominant metaphor of a *new frontier* or a *new world* (A. H. Gunkel & D. J. Gunkel, 1997; D. J. Gunkel & A. H. Gunkel, 2009), typically associated with a corresponding space constructed by the communicative affordances of the medium. So, thus, popular vernacular incorporates terms like "Radioland," "TV Land," and "cyberspace" as shared imaginary locations reified by the collective experience of technology. Much like geographically fixed worlds that humanity has conquered, these technologically enabled new worlds present imagined geographies that individuals hope to reinvent themselves in and tame at the same time. Evoking the metaphor of a *new world* or a *new frontier* suggests both an exercise in abandon and an exercise in power, as past inhabitants of new worlds traveled there to forget the past, start anew, and inevitably reshaped and were reshaped by new worlds in doing so. And so, the Internet is heralded as a new virtual homestead for community (e.g., Rheingold, 1993), an electronic frontier for democracy (e.g., Abramson, Arterton, & Orren, 1988; Arterton, 1987; Williams & Pavlik, 1994), or a new, alternative *terranova* for virtual gaming communities (D. J. Gunkel & A. H. Gunkel, 2009; Consalvo & Miller, 2009). As individuals greet new worlds with optimism, they are lured into forgetting about worlds of the past that let them down.

Several aptly perceive the allure of technological empowerment as having to do with sustaining popular fantasies of control, which promise ultimate autonomy and order over one's extended environment (Castoriadis, 1975/1987; Couldry & McCarthy, 2004; Morley, 2007). Ironically enough, individual autonomy is frequently only attainable through societal processes of order and control, which are also enabled by newer technologies (Robins & Webster, 1999). Still, employment of these metaphors represents an effort to ascribe "newness," and, by extension, to affirm the ability for this new frontier to be conquered, and thus controlled by masses feeling powerless in their contemporary environments, in a manner similar to that in which previous new worlds were inhabited and subsequently colonized. Yet it should be emphasized that autonomy and control are effected reflexively, through simultaneous processes of liberation and discipline connoted by the architectures of newer technologies. Thus, technological architectures that provide empowering options do so by multiplying layers of controlled choices people select from. Deleuze (1998) uses the metaphor of the highway, another metaphor popular in narratives of technological empowerment, to explain the process of controlled autonomy: "A control is not a discipline. In making highways, for example, you don't enclose people but instead multiply the means of control. I am not saying that this is the highway's exclusive purpose, but that people can drive infinitely and "freely" without being confined yet while still being perfectly controlled. This is our future" (p. 18). Similarly, new technologies suggest worlds upon which potential empowerment may be exercised. This may not be the sole function of these technologies, but it is the praxis reflective of fantasies of total control, sustained by individuals and their governments. To the extent that democracies grant absolute individual power or autonomy via a means of representatively elected elites of control, individuals may always experience a powerlessness that drives them to new democratic territories. The next few paragraphs describe the particular strand of relative powerlessness experienced by contemporary citizens.

Old and new democracy

Democracy is old. It is an old term with a long history and a variety of ethnic identities. Democracy is the majority: of the world's 192 countries, approximately 121 are electoral democracies (freedomhouse.org, accessed July 2008). Democracy is in danger, according to several reports of low voter turnouts in American and European nations. Democracy consists of cynical, apathetic, and disconnected electorates, according to the same contemporary rhetoric and research. This book traces what civic life is like in contemporary democracies where media play a central role in connecting the representatives to the public.

Too often we ask how media has failed democracy, or why citizens are no longer active in democracies. Responses are multiple and varied, but we rarely ask: does democracy need a reboot? Democracy is often treated as a static concept that we either practice effectively, live up to honorably, or are unable to attain. Democracy, however, is imaginary. It is an abstraction. It is based on an ideal, subject to many interpretations, which then influence how the abstraction is practiced by nation-centric political systems. As a concept, it is derived from the Greek *dimos* (public) and *kratos* (rule), which suggests that power lies with the people, a proposition that is both irrevocable and long-lasting. Without question, rule lies with the people, but when it comes to how that rule is exercised, the questions are many. Responses vary, depending on the unique economic, social, cultural, and political conditions of each society.

Thus, democracy is accepted as a negotiable abstraction, reified singularly by each society. If we accept that democracy as a concept is evolving and fluid, then the public or media (dis)engagement with the democratic system becomes consonant with that fluidity. An objective for the social scientist or the historian is to interpret the moment within the fluid progression that presents the contemporary or the current. And so the questions are: what is contemporary democracy, and what measure of power do individuals possess in contemporary democracies?

The conditions of contemporary democracy

The state of contemporary democracy has been a popular subject for academics, politicians, media pundits, and the public. Most discussions, regardless of the circle they may thrive in, are bound to reference one or more of the following trends: (a) nostalgia for past forms of political engagement, frequently wrapped in rhetoric that idealizes past iterations of a public sphere (e.g. Calhoun, 1992; Schudson, 1998); (b) limitations to civic involvement imposed by the representative democracy model, as it functions in a mass society resting on a capitalist economy (e.g. Coleman, 2005b; Habermas, 2004; Mouffe, 2000); (c) the aggregation of public opinion within representative democracy models through polling (e.g., Herbst, 1993); (d) declining civic participation through formal channels of political involvement (e.g., Carey, 1995; Hart, 1994; Putnam, 1996); and (e) the growth of public cynicism and disillusionment towards politics and the mass media (e.g., Cappella and Jamieson, 1996, 1997; Fallows, 1996; Patterson, 1993, 1996). These five tendencies characterize contemporary democracies, describe civic engagement in mass societies, and situate the media in the overall equation.

First, nostalgia for previous forms of civic engagement revolves around the merit of conversation, civic participation, and high levels of political engagement as reflective of a healthy democracy. The present era, characterized by reduced levels of conversation, political disinterest, and decreasing voter turnouts does not live up to civic performances of the past. Retrospective examinations of public engagement frequently evoke an ideal of the public sphere or public discourse, as located in democratic ideals of the Ancient Greek agora, the agora of the Roman Republic, conversations held in Enlightenment salons and coffeehouses, and, in general, the political habits and behaviors of our ancestors. The public sphere presents the notional locus within which civic deliberation and participation are situated, within a representative democracy. Still, we neglect the point that these past ideals frequently were exclusive and elitist, forming around spheres of gender, race, and class.

And yet arguments that connect civic engagement, public

discourse, and the present state of politics are frequently based on a premise that overestimates and romanticizes political activity in previous eras. For instance, Michael Schudson (1998), through historical analysis, demonstrated that American democracy was characterized by different models and periods of political activity, during which the average citizen was much less informed, educated, susceptible to persuasion, and active than in the contemporary era. Moreover, he has argued that public discourse is not the main ingredient, or "the soul of democracy," for it is seldom egalitarian, may be too large and amorphous, is rarely civil, and ultimately offers no magical solution to problems of democracy (Schudson, 1997).

The modern era citizen is frequently characterized as passive, cynical, and disconnected, but those trends are not specific to the present era, as several scholars have shown (e.g., Coleman, 2005b; Schudson, 1998). More importantly, for citizens of all eras, the propensity to be informed, and, thus, civically engaged, is not an idiosyncratic tendency, but, rather, a function of social, economic, and educational factors. As Delli Carpini (1999) has shown, most citizens, past and present, are generalists, meaning that they are drawn to general over specific knowledge, with some exceptions on matters of gender, race, and party politics. Within this context, more informed citizens are certainly more likely to be politically active, although activity is limited in a system that delivers few opportunities for direct communication with elites and sends conflicting messages about the value of direct citizen input.

Second, and relevant to burgeoning nostalgia, it must be understood that contemporary democracies are characterized by what is known as *the democratic paradox*; that is, the impossibility of practicing direct democracy in mass societies (Coleman, 2005b; Mouffe, 2000, 2005). Most contemporary societies are simply too large to practice models of direct democracy, thus adopting a model of representative democracy, wherein the public elects representatives to debate and manage civic affairs and governance. Several find that representative democracy requires homogeneity of public opinion and emphasis on majority rule, which preclude any possibility of true pluralism (e.g., Mouffe, 2000). Most political scientists subscribe to the more tempered viewpoint that, while civic engagement in representative democracy is not an impossibility, it is, nonetheless, a compromise.

Third, congruent to the challenge of direct communication in a representative democracy, is the trend to aggregate public opinion. Several conditions associated with the post-industrial era, including urbanization and the proliferation of mass communication have led government, politicians, and the mass media to rely on aggregations of public opinion obtained through polls. This trend, which Herbst (1993) refers to as "numbered voices," exchanges the individuality, detail, and authenticity of personal opinion on public affairs for a concentration of opinions that fit into predetermined question and answer sets reported in aggregation. The tendency to group and categorize public opinion, therefore, limits the opportunities for, and the scope of, discussion on public affairs, as citizens are not called upon to deliberate, but merely to report agreement or disagreement with certain questions. This phenomenon compromises the depth of the public discourse in ways unknown in past democracies, and restricts civic involvement with public affairs.

Fourth, all these trends are reflected in growing reluctance to participate in politics through formal or conventional channels of civic engagement, such as voting, community involvement, and volunteering. Despite the fact that the modern public sphere attempts to not draw distinctions based on gender, class, or race, the democratic model practiced in modern societies leaves little room for citizen involvement. Representative democracy involves citizens primarily as voters who elect officials to deliberate and make decisions for them. Efficacy of governance in a mass society is thus secured, but public deliberation of civic affairs is compromised. Compounding forces place additional restrictions. Carey (1995), for instance, argued that the privatizing forces of capitalism have created a mass commercial culture that has replaced the public sphere. Putnam (1996) attributed the disappearance of civic America to the omnipresent television, suggesting that television occupies all time previously devoted to civic affairs and induces passive outlooks on life. In the same vein, in a striking comparison of civic disengagement over the past 30 years, Delli Carpini

(2000) described young Americans as less trusting, less interested in politics or public affairs, less likely to feel a sense of obligation associated with citizenship, less knowledgeable about the substance and processes of politics, less likely to read a newspaper or watch the news, less likely to register to vote, less likely to participate in politics beyond voting, less likely to participate in similarly minded community organizations, and less likely to engage in traditional forms of civic engagement than their predecessors.

Finally, a parallel development of growing public cynicism and disillusionment with politics and the mass media keeps citizens from becoming actively involved with public affairs. Research conducted on the effects of cynicism consistently reveals that cynical language employed by politicians and the media, as well as the tendency to focus on insider goings-on instead of important issues, leads to skepticism about the impact political, media, and citizen action could have in improving public affairs (e.g., Cappella and Jamieson, 1996, 1997; Fallows, 1996; Patterson, 1993, 1996). As the prospect of civic participation influencing governance appears grim and as this skepticism is reinforced through negative or cynical coverage in the mass media, growing cynicism spreads in a spiraling manner (Cappella and Jamieson, 1996, 1997). Alternatively, Buckingham (2000) suggests that cynicism presents a strategy of self-presentation for civic publics, and especially the young, employed to mask perceived powerlessness and inability to impact the political sphere. The combination of these trends prescribes defined, and in most cases, limited civic roles for citizens. To the extent that these roles fail to produce civic contributions perceived as meaningful or impactful for the electorate, the average citizen is left with impressions of powerlessness, distrust, and lack of control.

A new(er) civic vernacular

Technology then presents a way to counter powerlessness by allowing individuals to propose new spaces, upon which newer, more empowering habits and relations may be cultivated. These social spaces present the sum of experiences past with interpretations present and potential of the future. They capture nostalgia and dissatisfaction with the past along with anticipation of the future through a mix of practices that are both *actual/given* and *potential*, thus reflecting "a locus of possibilities" (Lefebvre, 1974/1991, p. 191). Representing "at once a collection of *materials* (objects, things) and an ensemble of *matériel* (tools – and the procedures necessary to make efficient use of tools and of things in general)," these technologically enabled social spaces host civic activities marked by both convention and innovation. These civic activities develop around the praxis of the actual and the promise of the potential, combining internalized perceptions of *the political* with thoughts of what that which is political might signify in the future. This book then progresses by identifying and analyzing given and potential practices of digitally enabled democracies, viewing them both as an expression of distinct civic tendencies and as the tapestry upon which further tendencies form.

Chapter 2 situates modalities of civic expression in the historically sensitive private and public spatial binaries that characterize all democracies. The hierarchy of socio-cultural, political, and economic issues, institutions, and actors that colors a particular era also suggests a balance between public interest and private concerns, which organizes civic action, atomized and collective, developing within a democracy. It is frequently the tension between what is considered private and what is termed public that plots the civic territories along which citizens understand and practice their civic duties. These two conjoined abstractions, indefinable in their singularity and understood primarily in terms of how they mutually restrict and define each other, delineate the civic ecologies upon which civic habits, expectations, and conventions of democracies are formulated.

Chapter 2 also examines the dichotomy of public and private over time as it has shaped and been shaped by analytical thought, democratic praxis, and socio-economic realities. As a result, the shifting balances between what a society terms public and what it defines as private relate to common perceptions and practices of deliberation, political rationality, sociability, and civic representation and action in a democracy. Mapping the progress from solitude to the association that forms the basis of civic engagement and citizenship, private and public discursive spaces accommodate what Schement and Curtis (1997) have referred to as the tendencies and tensions of every age. Contemporary democracies are identified by: (a) increased commodification and privatization of public spaces, followed by a return to domestic or private spaces as political spaces; (b) a subsequent commodification of domestic and private spaces; and (c) a retreat to the realm of the social, as a way of reconciling the distance between public and private emerging polarities. These three trends set the stage for the current mode of civic engagement, representative of evolving perceptions of citizenship and malleable civic languages.

Convergent online technologies afford the social spaces upon which newer civic habits are tested out, and their particular civic potentialities are explicated in chapter 3. Technologies reorganize the balance between public and private spaces, thus suggesting an architecture upon which everyday routines are arranged. Chapter 3 is about the unique affordances of newer media technologies and how these connect to emerging civic habits. The concept of convergence presents a key construct around which the potentialities of online digital technologies are actualized. Convergence describes the confluence of technologies, practices, and spaces enabled by a variety of technologies, but it does not present a defining property of all technology, nor is it a property exclusive to technology. Information communication technologies are driven by a confluence of services and platforms, more so than other past or contemporary media technologies, which does not inherently democratize societal congregations of time and space, but it does render them more interconnected. On a primary level, the *convergence of technologies* modifies the means through which citizens become actualized. On a second level, a *convergence of spaces*, brought on by technology and various other systemic influences, rearranges the actual and imagined spaces upon which citizenship is practiced.

Finally, on a third level, a subsequent *convergence of practices* suggests a continuum of activities along which previously succinct categories of the social, cultural, economic, or political collapse and overlap. The multi-layered influence of convergence adjusts the architecture of what was previously recognized *as the political*, thus allowing new opportunities for engagement, but also creating dissonance in how citizens are internalizing their civic obligations, and how societal institutions are accounting for those citizen behaviors. As a result, declining voting turnouts and similar acts of political disinterest in conventional political habits are interpreted as cynicism or apathy, while other acts of political interest and engagement, such as blogging or "digging" news stories, do not register on the institutionalized radar of formalized political behaviors. Alternatively, reluctance to vote is frequently interpreted as ignorance or lack of concern, when in actuality it might represent a more complex expression of powerlessness in a networked political environment, the power of which extends well beyond the voting scope of the ordinary citizen. For centuries, we have understood the right to vote as the basic and ultimate recognition of democratic citizenship: a true honor bestowed upon all democratic citizens, several of whom may not have enjoyed this right in a non-democratic regime. However, as democratic regimes prevail and variations of parliamentary representation become the norm of practicing democracy, it is possible that the vote is perceived not as a privilege granted to citizens, but as a privilege citizens will grant to political parties. Possibly, as citizens and democracies evolve, the right to vote represents a primary need fulfilled, while secondary needs emerge, some of which fail to be met or even to register on contemporary democratic systems.

As new civic language and habits are formed, it is necessary to examine what it means to be a citizen in a converged and contemporary democracy. What makes a citizen is, of course, historically sensitive and never entirely definable. It was Aristotle who first recognized the absence and the impossibility of a single definition of citizenship, and, since then, models of citizenship have evolved and responded to economic, socio-cultural, and political schematics, as well as systems of ethics, morality, and religion. Complex as it is, citizenship suggests the ways in which civilians navigate democracy and become involved with the political.

Chapter 4 provides a historical overview of past models of

citizen engagement, to reveal a long history of imperfect citizen-ship. Still, our prolonged citizenship deficiencies demarcate ideals and suggest what it means to be a good citizen in the present era in ways not always cognizant of the contemporary context. This chapter examines the centrality of consumption in emerging civic behaviors, enabling individuals to claim citizenship through the possession of commodities and thus blurring demo-cratic and capitalist narratives. As individuals become civically emancipated through acts of consumption, cultural forms of citi-zenship are claimed to fulfill a sense of civic belonging, and these further fragment civil society into multiple, culturally oriented, and consumerism-driven citizen spheres. On a global level, these local cultures encounter the dynamics of the global market and politics, thus requiring cosmopolitan literacy of citizens previously civically actualized within the context of their home countries. Citizens thus employ media to survey a variety of hybrid or global spheres of subpolitical issues, representing personalized agendas of civic priorities, multicultural and transglobal. Through these monito-rial practices, emerging civic expressions originate in private and digitally equipped environments.

The emerging model of the digitally enabled citizen is liquid and reflexive to contemporary civic realities, but also removed from civic habits of the past. Most civic behaviors originate in private environments, and may be broadcast publicly to multiple and select audiences of the citizen's choosing and at the citizen's whim. The emerging political conscience is not collective, but privatized – both by virtue of its connection to consumer culture and in terms of the private spaces it occupies. The contemporary citizen adopts a personally devised definition of the political, and becomes politically emancipated in private, rather than public, spaces, thus developing a new civic vernacular.

These private expressions of citizenship that may or may not be broadcast in public bear variable democratizing consequences, that do not easily fit in deliberative or public governance models of the past. Understanding civic tendencies and tensions of the moment requires appreciating the molds that accommodate them, and those that do not. Online convergent technologies expand the sphere of information and opinion exchange, but they only do so for those possessing the prerequisite access and literacy levels. Even for the digitally equipped and literate, net-based information technologies do not guarantee communication that will be goal-oriented, reciprocal, and enriching. Many online conversations and pursuits are infotainment or entertainment-driven, consumption-oriented, or too specific to have a sizable democratizing impact.

Finally, the ongoing commercialization of online digital technologies is remediating newer media into simply newer versions of older media, thus expanding shopping catalogs for the consumer, but not affording democratic options for the citizen. Net-based technologies are susceptible to the systemic limitations that influence the democratizing potential of all media and have little ability to revive democratic ideals that never really existed in the first place.

But are we not misapplying the potential of online technologies, if we try to retrofit them into civic habits that no longer interest us? This is one of the questions visited in chapter 5. If the public sphere model proposes that the optimal way of practicing democracy is via organized, rational, and agreement-driven discussion taking place in commercial-free public spaces, then contemporary and digitally enabled civic habits must not represent democracy at its optimum. Or, alternatively, the public sphere model no longer works. This would require that we shift emphasis away from models of rational deliberation within representative democracy, and examine alternative formats of information and opinion exchange that develop in late modern democracies. Perhaps it is best to examine the geographies proposed by online technologies as hybrid spaces capable of hosting both public and private, commercial and public interest, political and social activities.

These newer civic habits that emerge in online hybrid spaces are examined in chapter 6, which proposes that all civic actions in contemporary democracies emanate from the locus of a private sphere. This private sphere is the focal point of all civic activity that develops, whether it remains within private confines or is broadcast to publicly positioned audiences and entities. Privately contained activities with a public scope, like online news reading, lurking in on political conversation, or following opinion leaders' blogs or tweets, take place within the locus of the private sphere. Publicly oriented activities, like posting a blog, sharing a political opinion, voting on or signing a petition to support a cause, or uploading exclusive news content on YouTube, are also increasingly enabled within the locus of a digitally equipped private sphere. In past iterations of democracy, these were all activities pursued in the public realm. In contemporary democracies, however, not only do these pursuits progressively emerge out of the private realm, but it is frequently necessary for the individual to return to the private realm in order to practice these newer civic habits with greater autonomy, flexibility, and potential for expression. This challenges the fundamental supposition that humans, in order to be social, and by consequence political, must possess public face: they must associate in the public realm. Via the affordances of technological environments, individuals fraternize from the privacy of their own spheres, practicing a form of networked yet *privé* sociality that is formulated within a private social sphere.

Net-based technologies permit the sociability of this private sphere. Online social networks, such as blogs and YouTube, collectively produced news aggregator sites, networks of online activism, all present popular and new civic habits, reflective of an electorate that is not apathetic, but is merely shifting its attention to different civic landscapes. Paradoxically enough, however, in order for the (fallen) public (hu)man, to paraphrase Sennett (1974), to rise again, the civic individual must fall back into the private sphere. Indeed, this is not far removed from Habermas' (1962/1989) or Arendt's (1970) discussion of the progression from privacy to publicity, in the sense that the subjectivity provided by the intimacy of the private sphere serves as "private preparation" of the autonomous individual for the public sphere (Dahlgren, 2009). In contemporary democracies, it is from the mobile and connected enclosure of this private cocoon that the individual directs atomized gestures of civic, social, cultural, economic, and multi-contextual natures to the rest of the world. Individuals retreat to the private sphere to escape from the conditions plaguing contemporary democracies into an environment they feel they possess greater control over.

Citizens recoil into their mobile and networked cocoons, thus communicating dislike for past public models of civic engagement, the nostalgia associated with them, the compromises and paradoxes of representative democracies, the aggregation and marketing of their publicly voiced opinions, and prescribed and formalized channels of civic engagement. They signal skepticism about the impact of conventional political process, and disillusionment with the public business of politics. I argue that in this private sphere citizens feel more secure in preserving their individual autonomy and the integrity of their civic identity, and in control of their civic fate.

Online technologies are not the first to enable mobile endeavors from the privacy of one's home. Williams (1974) introduced the concept of mobile privatization to describe the ways in which mass media allow mobility to be pursued from the privacy of one's home. Williams used the concept to explain the experience of witnessing from home and live, via television, events taking place at a different location. Mobile privatization could resolve the spatial tensions created by the conditions of modernity, for individuals asked to reconcile the spatial demands of work, the road, the automobile, and the home. The concept expresses the paradox of media-enabled mobility in societies that valued home-based private living. Spigel (1994, 2001) used the concept to explain how television introduces elements of mobility in domestic spaces, thus enabling both a retreat to suburbia and a newer form of media-centered community. Du Gay, Hall, Janes, Mackay, and Negus (1997) evoked the concept of mobile privatization to understand the ways in which a social technology, like the Walkman, permits individuals to manage public and private boundaries, while at the same time communicating in a variety of symbolic contexts. Hay (2003) re-deployed the concept as privatized mobility, to examine the domestic sphere as a sphere of self-governance, organized through multiple technologies.

Williams (1983) returned to the term *mobile privatization* and used it to talk about "private and self-enclosed individuals," living in private small-family units, in the midst of "unprecedented mobility of such restricted practices." He intended the term as descriptive of a sociality, exercised through the privatized mobility of enclosed spheres. The term captures the irony and poignancy of being social within private surroundings, as a way of reconciling, on the personal level, the conflicting traffic flows of modernity. The contemporary equivalent of the privately mobile social actor can be located in the iPod-wearing individual, whom Apple commercials hail as a displaced yet connected urban *flâneur*, maneuvering upon neon-colored blank backdrops. Similarly, individuals recording or simulcasting concerts and other live experiences via their mobile devices are attempting similar exercises in mobile privatization, aimed at reconciling disparities between their public and private spheres of communication. In an even more complex layering of public and private priorities, the digitally connected attendees of the Obama Election Night event related in the introduction to this chapter, were attempting to manage their private spheres from the public location of the event, while at the same time participating in an event that hailed them as private citizens celebrating collectively in the mass and somewhat impersonal setting of a grand, large-scale event. Through the use of mobile devices, attendees were seeking to maintain the coherence of their distinct private spheres while sharing the experience of a public event, organized within the private parameters of an enclosed space. And many others, connecting from home or mobile locations of temporary privacy, similarly seek to balance a variety of conflicting demands, within a greater civic environment characterized by cynicism and limited accessibility to elected officials and political power.

These technologically enabled private spheres sustain fantasies of control for contemporary citizens who are dissatisfied with the conditions of the public civic environments they inhabit. The citizen in post-industrial, late modern democracies is not alone. But, s/he is occasionally isolated, as sociability is defined both via acts of association and acts of withdrawal. If we think of democracy as a way of resolving individuals' complex relationship between public and private, then the private sphere is the locus from which individuals negotiate their relationship with the status quo of democracy. Democracy has always presented a way of reconciling public with private, whether that be private interest with public, private motivation with public affairs, private reflection with public association, or protection of private rights and the guarantee of freedom and equality for all publics.

Think back on Eliasson's *Parliament of Reality* and imagine a similar space, enabled by technology, and evoked by individuals so as to permit retreat from the hubbub of busy public spaces we daily occupy. This private space is constructed so as to denote distance from the public realm and connote difference from the imperatives pursued by the same individuals, in public. This temporary privacy permits disconnection, but to interpret retreat to a private sphere as an act of social disconnect would be missing the point of both *Parliament of reality* and a similarly enabled private sphere. The retreat to the private sphere is effected so as to sustain existing relationships and create new ones. Technology becomes the architecture of the new that sustains and is sustained by newer relationships and social habits that emerge. In this book, I argue that citizens feel more powerful in negotiating their place in democracy via the nexus of a private sphere. This retreat to the private sphere is an act of dissent, and as such is a political act. The subsequent negotiation of place is also political, as the negotiation of place always has been. Is it democratizing? To be discussed.

2

Public and Private Expression in Contemporary Democracies

Political governance is defined by the ways in which it allows public and private entities to interact. The economic, socio-cultural, and political texture of systems is woven as public and private concerns intersect to form distinctions between what is termed private and what is commonly understood to be public. More than organizing categories, *public* and *private* serve to qualify and distinguish manifested choices in everyday life. Much like all constructs characterized by bipolarity, what is important is not just the territory marked by public and private, but the distance and potential disparity between how public and private are situated in societal groupings. It is the tension between these two that sets the stage for political interaction, and reminds all of the public imperatives and private pursuits that democracies are in place to preserve and guarantee. "Public and private, *sic et non*," Jean Bethke Elshtain (1997) remarks, and continues: "Only in the space opened up by the ongoing choreography of these categories can politics exist – or at least any politics that deserves to be called democratic" (p. 180).

The distinction between public and private is elusive, as it is culturally formed and sensitive to historical context (e.g., Sennett, 1974; Weintraub & Kumar, 1997). The tendency to often use the two terms in ways that are more self-referential and less universal further contributes to the lack of definitional consistency. Still, the distinction between public and private is defined by the reason *why* we wish to draw the distinction in the first place (Geuss, 2001). Without a set of purposes, values, and questions that setting this distinction will serve, employing the private/public binary as an analytical tool bears no merit. For the purposes of the present argument, the analytical context here is that of civic engagement in a digital age, wherein the objective is to understand how shifting borders of private and public influence how citizens interpret, internalize, and practice their civic duty. This chapter provides a historical overview of the most common uses of the terms public and private, with a focus on how they reorganize discourses surrounding civic engagement and citizenship, which present core themes of this volume. Having done so, attention is devoted to how the distinction between public and private applies to contemporary democracy by explicating three dominant themes: (a) the commodification of privacy and private domains, (b) the privatization of public spaces and the use of private space as political space, and (c) a trichotomy posed by the interjection of the social into the public/private binary continuum.

Like most binary distinctions, that of public and private can help organize analytical thought and interpret behavioral patterns, but employing this distinction can be both illuminating and restrictive. In theory, the conceptual boundaries of public and private help us understand economic, political, legal, moral, and many other questions of cultural relevance, but in practice, they are frequently subjectively reappropriated to fit the demands of everyday routines. This analysis visits the conceptual themes of public and private as they enable and confine theory and practice, with the ultimate goal of providing a better understanding of the tension between the two, rather than providing absolute definitions. Because conceptual clarity about what is public and what is private is historically and culturally sensitive, and ultimately rests with the individual, analytical thought can be aided by understanding the forces creating tension and compatibility between private and public ways of thinking and acting. It is this tension between disparity and closeness that eventually motivates thought and practice that resides within public or private boundaries, or somewhere in between.

The dichotomy of public and private over time

Public and private may be defined, on the simplest level, on the basis of mutual exclusivity. Thus, public is that which does not remain private, and thus can be shared in *common*; is associated with the greater *public good*; can serve as a *mask* or fiction for private desires for power and position; can suggest a way for members of a public to become associated and effect action; and can exist within or outside the realm of the *state*. Conversely, private is that which does not become public, and thus remains under private *ownership*, in the realm of the *personal* or *domestic*, possibly considered *unofficial*, and involving actions and consequences structured around the *self*. Most discourses, whether theoretical or applied, evoke these terms in identifying the boundaries around which perceptions of public and private are formed. Weintraub (1997) describes the public/private distinction as "not unitary, but protean, [comprising] not a single opposition, but a complex family of them, neither mutually reducible nor wholly unrelated" (p. 2). Thus, separating the two terms, even if just for definitional purposes, conjures a variety of constructs, which are conceptually distinct, yet overlap in both theory and practice.

Weintraub (1997) puts forth two criteria for discerning private and public which capture the etymological denotations of the terms with adequate, yet not distracting, focus on their connoted meanings. Employing the criteria of *visibility* and *collectivity*, private is defined in contrast to public as: (a) what is hidden or withdrawn versus what is open, revealed, or accessible; or (b) what is individual, or pertains only to an individual, versus what is collective or affects the interests of a collectivity of individuals. This individual/collective distinction can, by extension, take the form of a distinction between part and whole (of some social collectivity) (Weintraub, 1997, p. 5). Employing the criteria of visibility and collectivity enables one to examine the parameters and consequences of the private/public distinction across analytical planes that are diverse and interconnected.

Public and private boundaries define how individuals organize their everyday ecologies and relate to others, and have been the subject of considerable philosophical thought. The earliest mentions of the term private are associated with private property, and can be traced back to the works of Plato and Aristotle, who saw private property as a more efficient way of managing affairs that could not be administered in common. Plato, in various works, examined the implications of land ownership as private property and advocated in part for communal ownership of land among rulers of the state as a means of avoiding conflict, and later on for private ownership for individually held land and houses, as long as that did not exceed the state-allowed level of private holdings. Aristotle in turn saw private ownership of land as a means of ensuring that men may enjoy the fruits of their labor and as a motive for being productive, although he, too, advocated some restrictions on private ownership, primarily on inheritances. On the other hand, the work of Plato sets the foundation, whereas Aristotle more sharply defines the distinction between public and private as a division between two distinct institutional domains, the private domain of the household (οἶκος) and the public domain, located in public space (δῆμος) and involving the management of public affairs for the greater good of the *city-state* (πόλις). The term *polis* can be loosely interpreted as a city-state, but it mainly denotes a form of social organization and less the urban and administrative functions that the term *city-state* may connote at present.

For the Greek and the Roman philosophers, emphasis was placed on presence in the public arena, public affairs, and leading a good life. The term public was thus associated with principles of governance, democracy, and deliberation. Conversely, private delineated the locus of the home and related activities. Thus, the public man emerged as a citizen of the world, a member of a civil society with civic duties. Within this context, private property ownership signified status and granted private individuals participation rights and greater power leverage in public life. At the nadir of the Roman period, Christianic values positioned private man before God and redefined the essence of what it means to lead a good life. This marked a departure from the Greco-Roman politically based definitions of Virtue (*aretê*) to morally constructed and religious interpretations of Virtue as piety. As religious discourse dominated the private sphere and permeated private life, it, along with concurrent political and economic developments, reframed the contours of public and private behaviors (e.g., Ariés, Veyne, Duby, & Goldhammer, 1987–91). During this period, private began to specifically delineate that which is privately owned and impenetrable by public vision. This effectively extended the public/private binary beyond the political to domains that are social, cultural, and, in general, behavioral, thus suggesting multiple directions for analytical thought which had, up until that point, treated this mostly in its political context. Consequently, the construct of the citizen, previously defined within a strictly political framework, became associated with social, cultural, and national territories.

Natural Law theory – from its roots in Aristotle and the Stoics, to religiously associated incarnations of theory (early Christianity, Islam, then Roman Catholicism), to Hobbes' Natural Law and more contemporary understandings of human life, rights, and goodness – is invested in the public/private distinction, and how the distinction delineates the boundaries for human behavior. Natural Law theorists have followed a complex journey through the works of Aristotle, to Pufendorf and Hobbes, to Locke and, finally, Hutchenson to map out the citizen figure as the "autonomous agent, who can act following the law of nature, by assessing the possible or actual consequences of his own and others' actions," thus rejecting "the figure of the citizen as the *dominus*, the property-holder and the master, by making the link between private acquisition and public rights contingent rather than necessary" (Gobetti, 1997, p. 129). Past and contemporary profiles of individuals as *political animals* are structured on the basis of how public behaviors are differentiated from private ones, and the degree of autonomy and power associated with the public and private spheres respectively.

Also important here is the close connection of people to the state that formulates during the same time and the three ideological shifts that sequentially enabled it: (a) the growing influence of Republican thought, (b) the Protestant Reformation, and (c) the development of political community around "ethnic, cultural and localist solidarities" (Calhoun, 1997, p. 78). Republicanism, as conceived and practiced in Ancient Greece and Rome, and then revived in modern Europe, placed the public at the center of democracy connecting public deliberation to communal decision-making, thus granting citizens access to power and agency. The range of citizens who were included in the public varied and depended on private property ownership and gender-, class-, and race-related exclusionary rhetoric. Still, the public was the deliberative vehicle for democratically extracting discourses out of the private realm and granting them legitimacy by locating them in the public realm. The Protestant Reformation captured the religious influence on the notion of public governance, as articulated by "theocratic communities of the patristic era" (Calhoun, 1997, p. 78). The emphasis on religiosity shifted attention from the *public* to the *people*, as the governing entity of the polity, which was convened more explicitly on the basis of shared civic and religious duty. Finally, communities structured around localized culture and ethnicity signaled the emergence of the *other* as political opposite or ally. Because the other is frequently defined in relation to discourses that elude the public sphere and remain in private, this ideological shift marked the process through which these discourses became integrated into Republican or Protestant-influenced models of public deliberation and governance.

In modern Western thought then, these developments underlined how the criteria of visibility and collectivity, around which the public/private distinction is assembled, frame models of democratic deliberation and governance that have emerged. However, not all human action is civically motivated, although still capable of civic repercussions. Therefore, social and political thought observes the private/public distinction within the context of a democracy, but is obligated to understand how the distinction manifests itself in a set of interconnected realms of human thought and action. These are frequently organized under the following four groupings: the liberal-economic model, the republican-virtue or classical approach, the sociability focus, and the private/domestic vs. public / greater social order distinction (e.g., Weintraub, 1997; Schwarzmantel, 2003). The liberal-economic model is prevalent in most policy discussions and underlines the distinction between the market economy and state involvement. The Republican or classical model places emphasis on the public or the people as a governing entity distinct from the state or the market. The focus on sociability examines social actions articulated in the private and public realms, the ways in which social actions traverse between these two realms, and the civic footprint left along the way. Finally, feminism and other theory frequently examines the domestic sphere as the private sphere, which marks a distinction between the family unit and the greater social and political whole.

The *liberal-economic* model is influenced by neoclassical economic theory that specifies specific roles for the market and the state in models of economic development. Employing the private/public distinction so as to delineate the government/state as the public sector and independently owned or managed companies and organizations as the private sector, this model tends to place capitalist analysis at odds with a social utilitarian approach. The private sector emphasizes rational thought and self-regulated behavior as ways of achieving the commonly shared goals of perfect competition, market equilibrium, and supply-and-demand efficiency. At the opposite extreme, the public sector frequently accounts for irrationality in human thought and behavior, structured on the general premise of the inability of markets to function in a manner that efficiently caters to all societal and economic strata.

Employing the private/public distinction to understand state and market differences in public policy situates the two sectors in opposition, and defines the distance between the two as irreconcilable. At the same time, it simplifies discussion of options that are possible via publicly owned vs. privately managed entities. This binary opposition is articulated notably by economic thinkers like John Locke and Adam Smith at the private end, and Hobbes and Bentham at the public end, is defended by varying schools of economic and political thought, and reinforced by the tendency to locate all economic debates around the bipolar ends of private and public. All points of view concern the process through which conflict between interests of the self and interests of the whole is harmonized, whether this is effected via the "invisible" hand of market forces or the "visible" hand of government involvement. Within this context, the assumption that the public and private sectors are not compatible is cultivated. In contrast, a public policy conversation that took place somewhere in the middle of that continuum could enable models of enlightened capitalism or a moderate social welfare state (e.g., Bauman, 2007a & b; Sennett, 2006).

The *Republican* or *classical* model identifies public as associated with action that is mostly political, whereas private life is relegated mostly to the domain of the family and the home. Weintraub (1997) aptly points out that the words *public* and *private* are Roman, while the conceptualization is Greco-Roman. Indeed, while discussion of private and public life is founded on both Ancient Greek and Roman philosophy, the Greeks use terms like the *polis* or the *Commons* (δῆμος) to refer to public life, and the term *home* (οἶκος), in denoting firm locations for public and private discourses. The Greco-Roman traditions solidify the concepts of a self-governing public and sovereignty, thus situating citizens as the political actors and shared rules as the *modus operandi* of a democracy. As these notions succumb to the influence of religiosity and morality and re-emerge in modernity, emphasis is placed on civil society as the locus where self-interested individuals convene to establish sovereignty and function as citizens. In this context, dominant thinkers contribute to the philosophical construction of civil society: Hobbes by emancipating opinion, identifying with conscience and freeing it from religion; Locke by emphasizing reason and criticism as key elements of informed and educated opinion; Rousseau by re-establishing the importance of the general will of the people and establishing consensus; and Kant by proposing the public sphere as the means through which the conflicting private wills of rational people could be brought into harmony. Within this context, Hegel questions the ability of public opinion to function outside the confines of prejudice, ideology, and irrationality; Marx further problematizes it as a mask for bourgeois class interests.

The focus on rationality and the potential for the irrationality of public opinion define the construct of civil society, as they do the market, which operates concurrently and in contrast to the political sphere demarcated by civil society. Liberalism is established as the founding philosophy of the civil society, advocated by public intellectuals like de Tocqueville and Mill, who recognize the disharmony triggered by capitalism and accept relative, but perfect, freedom of action. Civil society is conceptualized as distinct from the market or the bureaucracy of the state, either of which carry the potential of suppressing the will and actions of atomized individuals operating collectively.

A focus on *sociability* explicates how private and public spheres provide the stages across which social behaviors of the individual unfold. These social performances are enabled and restricted by cultural and historical conventions of what is termed private and what is considered public. The work of Philippe Ariés presents a common reference point for scholars, as his *Centuries of Childhood* (1962) provides a historically influenced overview of the ways in which private and public surroundings influence family communication patterns and related social roles. The work of Ariés and collaborators in the Private Life series (1987–91, 1993) traces how religious, ideological, and economic tendencies and tensions delineate private and public planes for activity, thus imposing felt rules on how individuals across history and culture experience and practice private and, by default, public life. The works help contextualize modernity as the result of a long and complex conversation between religion, political philosophy, the economy, and individual self-interest. The antitheses depicted are present in other seminal works that problematize the tensions between public life and modernity. For Tönnies, the distinction between private and public helps construct the conceptual foundation for the concepts of *Gemeinschaft* and *Gesellschaft*, which capture modes of solitary and collective existence, respectively, that are both historically and culturally sensitive.

The ways in which modernity simultaneously enables solitude and complicates togetherness represent important themes for scholars who employ the public/private distinction to understand this. For instance, Goffman (1959, 1963, 1971) focuses on situations created by modern settings to understand, from a dramaturgical perspective, how behavior evolves across public and private social planes. Gans (1962, 1967), on the other hand, locates these tensions in the urban setting, and examines how the architectural structures of modernity restrict and suggest ways of existing politically and socially for individuals. Sennett (1974) compares and contrasts past and present modes of social and political activity to argue for the demise of the ability to exist, connect, and express oneself in public. This list is by no means exhaustive, but rather, it is exemplary of thinkers who refer back to the public/ private distinction to situate and comprehend socially motivated behaviors.

Feminist theory is influenced by these works and others that contrast the private/domestic domain with the behaviors and roles endorsed by the public domain. Within this realm of analytical thought, the domestic sphere is viewed as a feminized space, from which women may exert and negotiate any amount of power or agency afforded them by the current socio-cultural setting. Within this context, the public/private distinction becomes gendered, relegating females to the domestic sphere and assigning males as active members of the public sphere. The public/private divide operates as part of an ideological apparatus that minimizes the significance of the domestic sphere, and serves to conceal or confine behaviors occurring within it. Public life then involves masculinized public space and routines, whereas private life involves the feminized locale of domesticity. The work of Marx and Engels explicates how class oppression and female subordination are reinforced through the dominant ideology of capitalism. Pateman (1989) builds on this analysis to make the point that essentially all feminist theory is about the separation of public and private.

Different schools of feminist thought engage the private/public distinction in variant ways, although most begin by problematizing the relegation of women to space that is private, and thus depoliticized. Marxist feminism then connects female oppression to the rhetoric of capitalism, to ways in which capitalism employs the private/public binary. Radical feminism emphasizes male and female difference and prioritizes female communities as a means of advancing female agendas, which in some ways either dispenses altogether with the public/private binary or employs it in a manner that supports female rights (e.g., MacKinnon, 1987, 1989). For post-structuralist feminists, private and public present physical and linguistic boundaries upon which cultural perceptions of what a society terms *female* are constructed. For post-feminists, gender is performative, more than biologically or socially constructed, and thus dualisms posited by private and public territories are typically analyzed as restrictive of the ways in which gender is experienced and enacted (e.g., Butler, 1990; Haraway, 1991).

This volume is concerned with civic engagement, and how modes of civic engagement traverse across public and private planes of activity as newer technologies for political participation emerge. Therefore, I do not delve into exhaustive reviews of the liberal-economic model, the Republican-classical model, sociability, and feminist theory. Still, it is necessary to extract analytical concepts from these streams of thought that help in examining contemporary civic engagement. These four themes, articulated by Weintraub (1997) but evoked by most scholars considering the impact of the public and private separation (e.g., Benhabib, 1992; Calhoun, 1997; Livingstone, 2005; Silver, 1997; Wolfe, 1997), inform how the separation of private and public influences political activity. Resting on classical liberalism and blending the work of sociologists like Simmel and Goffman, Silver (1997) argues that the domain of the private is created as *personal*, in contrast to the *impersonal* domain of the public, which contains activities intrinsic to the economic and political order of contemporary democracies. In the same vein, and drawing from the Republican-classical model and literature on sociability, Wolfe (1997) concludes that "[neither] Goffman nor Habermas makes a completely convincing case for either the private or the public, which suggests that . . . both are essential to the way we live now – and to each other as well" (p. 188). Calhoun (1997) connects these analytical threads to underline the dual existence of individuals in contemporary democracies, through the administration of private affairs and through their public roles. Within this context, public and private are parallel, implying that "the private is simultaneously that which is not subject to the purview of the state and that which concerns personal ends distinct from the public good, the *res publica* or matters of legitimate public concern" (p. 81).

Still, the foundation is laid out for the public and private distinction to be invoked in discussions of civic engagement and public administration. Definitions of public and private are susceptible to historical and cultural context, as well as the linguistic context within which they are employed. Livingstone (2005) synthesizes these tendencies by proposing a reflexive typology, inclusive of past theory and practice of public and private, but also sensitive to the realities of contemporary democracies. Thus, the public/private distinction revolves around and adapts to the following key oppositions or sets of questions: (a) *profit*, which includes questions of interest: who benefits? (b) *participation*, which includes questions of social relations, common culture, and in/exclusion; and (c) *governance*, which includes questions of visibility, rights, responsibilities, and protection (p. 169). This typology permits the understanding of both past and current socio-political organizations, and allows a discussion of fundamental shifts in how the private/public distinction is theorized and applied.

Within this organizational framework, for questions of *profit*, *public* may be defined as intended for the public interest, good, or sector, whereas *private* refers to the commercial or commodified, acting out of self-interest or for the private sector (Livingstone, 2005). For audiences and publics, profit and non-profit-driven imperatives intertwine and suggest a variety of civic activities that occupy planes that may be private, public, or both. In the same typology and regarding questions of *participation*, public is understood as enabling connection and sharing in culture and deliberation, reflective of "civic engagement" and "public opinion", whereas private implies withdrawal or isolation (Livingstone, 2005). Thus, public and private realms are constructed and occupied so as to differentiate engagement from disengagement. Finally, for questions related to *governance*, public implies accountability and transparency and is inclusive of behaviors that take place in the "front stage" or "public eye," whereas private is equal to privacy, "backstage" behavior, and lack of surveillance, and connotes privacy rights (Livingstone, 2005). Rather than examining the public/private distinction as a linear binary, this typology allows a more complex discussion of the multiple planes of socio-economic activity on which private and public domains overlap or separate. These planes, across which public/private boundaries intersect with objectives related to profit, governance, and participation, form potential *lifeworlds*, or socio-culturally structured environments where individual experiences materialize (Habermas, 1981/1987).

Moreover, through this theorization of public and private, it is possible to embark on a discussion of how concepts central to this volume, such as the citizen, online digital media, and spheres of civic activity, materialize and develop across overlapping sectors. Employing this typology, this chapter identifies themes that locate the dichotomy of public and private in modern democracies.

The dichotomy of public and private at present

On questions relating to profit, participation, and governance organized across public and private domains, three dominant themes emerge and characterize how the dichotomy of public and private materializes in modern democracies. The first theme brings attention to the private realm as a personal domain presently contested by profit-driven objectives, thus leading to a potential commodification of *privacy*. This has an effect on how citizens understand civic roles to be enacted in private and public places. A subsequent second theme concerns the *privatization of public space* and the retreat to the home as space that is not commodified and that can possibly serve as non-commercial, political space. Finally, a third theme involves the rejection of both public and private spaces for the pursuit of a malleable space in between, characterized by activity that is *social* at heart, but that could embed political/civic merit and consequences.

Public and private space: The privatization of public space and the (return to the) home as political space

Radical feminists coined the phrase "the personal is political" in asserting the presence of a feminist agenda in the public arena. Borrowed from a 1969 essay authored by Carol Hanisch, the phrase gained notoriety as it was employed to relay the complexity of female oppression and to grant a political dimension to the suppression of the female perspective experienced in the private/ domestic sphere. Reflective of a rhetoric aimed at giving a public voice to marginalized issues and groups, the phrase often reflects the sentiment of the underrepresented. In this context, and with full appreciation for the cultural *gravitas* of the phrase, I employ it to describe a retreat from public spaces of political expression to private spaces of civic engagement, capable of supporting and broadcasting individual opinion on public *and* private affairs, to public spheres and audiences of variable size and impact. The path from private to public and then back to private is complicated, and is connected to the historical progression of public and private territory. So let's examine the points it crosses.

Historically and culturally sensitive, this path is marked by the intersection of public and personal with questions of *profit* and *participation*. Still the premise of this argument lies in the idea that public space has somehow ceased to be a meaningful space for the expression of political identity.

Public space presents one of the fundamental requirements of democracy. Democracy is founded on the premise of inclusion of all diverse viewpoints. Deliberation is central to a democracy, for it creates the mode through which private expression enters the public realm. Some have argued, compellingly, that conversation is not the essence of a democracy (Schudson, 1997, and from a different standpoint, Mouffe, 2005), but that does not necessarily displace deliberation from a central position in any democracy, for deliberation presents the medium through which public and private expression and opinion are negotiated. Public space simultaneously enables and validates deliberation by providing democratic conversation with a meeting place that is accessible to all. In political theory, this common meeting place that is devoted to deliberation that forwards democratic ideals is *the public sphere*. Like all constructs, the public sphere is developed by the human intellect to describe a state of deliberation. It does not exist in actuality and remains elusive to the human senses. Seeking to fix it to a historical point is an ill-fated pursuit; as a construct, it is reified only in the public consciousness. It is possible to point to occasions of public deliberation in trying to conceptually define the construct, and that is what the modern architect of the concept, Jürgen Habermas, does in referring to ancient Greco-Roman spheres of deliberation as reflective of public sphere formations. Habermas (1962/1989, 1991) argues that civic participation in past

eras was aspirant to modes deliberative of equality and complexity found in Ancient Greco-Roman agoras, and eighteenth- and
nineteenth-century coffee houses and literary salons in Europe.
A Westernized approach to political participation, the public
sphere presents deliberative space in Western democracies where
self-interest morphs into public opinion and, potentially, political
action. The public sphere is enabled by social spaces that facilitate
public gatherings, and it is Habermas' argument that in modern
and post-modern democracies that public space is commercialized
and thus can no longer serve the interests of the people, as those
interests are formulated distinctly from the interests of the state
and the private sector. The commodification of public space by
commercial interest, the mass media, and the rhetoric of public
relations and advertising transforms spheres of civic engagement
to spaces of commercial exchange. As the purity of public deliberation is compromised by the private sector and/or the state, it is no
longer possible for the public sphere to exist in public space as a
distinct entity.

Critics and proponents of Habermas' viewpoint (e.g., Calhoun,
1992) elaborate on the finer points of this argument, and the
viability of the public sphere as a core construct of the information age is examined later on in this volume. For the sake of the
present argument, it is important to focus on public space over
the public sphere. Analytical thought frequently debates whether
a public sphere ever truly existed, but in fairness to the true spirit
of Habermas' argument, this misses the point. What is important
is not whether the public sphere ever was, but, rather, that the
conditions necessary for it to ever *be* have become extinct. The
public sphere existed as an abstract ideal in the public consciousness, as that public consciousness was experienced across various
historical eras. But the public sphere, abstract or tangible, requires
public space to exist, and Habermas' point is that the public space
that previously enabled the collective sharing of a public sphere no
longer exists.

Habermas argues that the absence of purely deliberative, un-
commercialized public space has had a narcotizing effect on the
public sphere and on political activity in general. As a possible

consequence, political activity is diffused into smaller, marginal or semi-marginal spheres of civic interaction, or *counter-publics* (Fraser, 1992), which Habermas (1992) recognizes in later work. These counter-publics locate public activity outside the public sphere, thus overcoming previous exclusions of women, non-property-owners, and underrepresented groups from public life. For some, multiple counter-publics of variable size, rhetoric, and impact, operating collaboratively or in opposition, form the political texture of post-industrial democracies. This model explains the rise of political and marginal movements despite or in opposition to prevalent models of ideological hegemony, and leads to the formation of identity politics as the *sui generis* of contemporary democracies. A contested term, *identity politics* broadly describes social movements that no longer require collective action reflective of the interest of a social group – they revolve more around personal identity and sense-making of cultural information. Melucci (1994, 1996), among others, contended that, since the late 1970s, emerging social conflicts in complex societies have raised cultural challenges to the dominant language, rather than expressing themselves through political action. Although Melucci implied that such language shifts are ineffectual, the point is that collective action can no longer be overtly measured, but is still present in the creative proclamation of cultural codes. Thus civic activity is performed not necessarily through focusing on traditional political issues, but rather by shifting the cultural ground.

The underlying objective, pursued by both the public sphere and counter-publics, is that of *plurality*, the absence of which Arendt (1958) identifies as the primary characteristic of modern democracies. Plurality is associated with diversity of perspective, which is possible but not guaranteed with inclusion or broad participation. Plurality is premised upon open participation, performed in activities pursued and shared in public, and entails the forgoing of private life and self-interest. In this sense, commercialized public spaces obstruct plurality and displace public activity to private realms where the possibility of potential plurality is also doomed. According to Sennett (1974), this interaction of "public geography and capitalism" results in synchronous "withdrawal from the public into the family," and "confusion about the materials of public appearance, a confusion which could be turned into a profit" (p. 20). The commercialization of public spaces not only dislocates public activity, but also creates a paradox for the modern individual who is offered public spaces that possess *visibility*, but *do not* enable *collectivity*. It is this sentiment of personal isolation in the midst of ultimate public visibility that captures the political mood of contemporary citizens who are suspended in these public spaces with the absence of what Arendt (1970) terms the "in-between," that is, "the specific and usually irreplaceable in-between which should have been formed between the individual and his fellow men" (p. 4).

In his exploration of the historical and cultural circumstances that brought on the "fall of public man," Sennett (1974) terms spaces where this bond is absent as "dead public spaces." It should be emphasized that the fall of the public individual to domains that are private pertains less to a personal lack of political interest and more to the gradual relocation of political interest in domains that are private, and thus more intimate. Dead public space presents the most concrete reason why "people seek out on intimate terrain what is denied them on more alien ground," thus mapping a return to private space in pursuit of the *in-between* bonds shared in collective existence (p. 15). In Sennett's argument (1974), as in Arendt's (1958, 1970), the transformation of the public domain is the result of slow and gradual changes to behaviors termed public and thus allowed access to the public domain.

The combined influences of philosophical, moral, economic, cultural, social, and political changes advanced through the liberal-economistic model, the republican-virtue or classical approach to politics, transformations of socially desirable sociability across public and private domains, and the ongoing renegotiation of the boundaries between domestic/private and greater social order / public sphere, have gradually led to the present binary of public and private. The foundation for our contemporary *lifeworld* was laid in the eighteenth and nineteenth centuries, as the cumulative impact of previous influences was absorbed, thus placing, in Sennett's terms, our past much closer to our historical present.

The progression towards a more intimate society was set in motion as Victorians became more cognizant of the impressions formed by their public and private behaviors through the advent of psychoanalysis as a discipline. Concurrently, as private life choices became a way to validate the credibility of political belief in the nineteenth century, the private further imposed itself on the public. The Victorian era also witnessed the concealment of public emotion as a way of preserving the privacy of one's character (Sennett, 1974). The result was an array of public behaviors that emphasized passive observation, voyeurism, and avoidance of interaction as individuals traversed public domains of an urban nature. These survival strategies enabled the transition from the *Gemeinschaft* principles of rurally based association to the *Gesellschaft* ways of urban industrialized living.

While this progression was traced in the historical overview of the public/private binary in greater detail, specific elements of it are emphasized here to connect a crisis in public life associated with industrialism and post-industrialism to a retreat to the private sphere for personal expression, be that social, cultural, or political. As a result, the public individual, dislocated, turns to the private arena, to be left alone in exercising his/her civic duty. But the private realm is no longer what it used to be either, and the complexities of this retreat are explicated next.

Privacy as commodity

The criteria of visibility and collectivity, employed to define private and public earlier in this chapter, delineate as private the domain inaccessible to the greater public. This domain pertains solely to the individual and little beyond that. General as this distinction may be, it is reflective of the ways in which political, cultural, and social activities traverse across public and private. In modern democracies, capitalism challenges the imperceptibility of the private realm, as information about decision-making and behaviors that occur in the private realm increasingly becomes a tradable commodity. Mediated communication complicates matters in information societies, as a variety of information-related goods and services contribute to economic productivity, and are produced and consumed in the private realm of home-related activities (Bell, 1981; Schement & Lievrouw, 1989). Within this environment, advanced data-mining technologies transform personal behaviors, consumer and non-consumer-oriented, into commodifiable entities (e.g., Gandy, 1989; Hamelink, 2000; Turow, 2001).

These behaviors carry a variety of orientations, although they usually form around the spheres of entertainment, consumption, and information processing, often blending activities previously categorized as social, cultural, or political into the vast multimedia category of infotainment (Castells, 2000; Schement & Curtis, 1997). The home, the socio-cultural locus of the family, becomes permeated with commercially oriented imperatives, resulting in what Lasch (1977) has termed "the family besieged." Compounded by the growing convergence of household and consumer culture, the private sphere of the family is colonized by commercial interest and further privatized. In this context, consumerist rhetoric is blended with political, social, and personal conversation to produce what some have termed a "democracy of the microwave" (Kumar, 1997, p. 225). Information communication technologies further augment these tendencies by enabling locational surveillance of private behaviors through mobile phones, digital video recording systems and other household devices, and challenging the meaning of private property within regulatory frameworks that do not legally address privacy in its entirety (Gandy & Farall, 2008; May, 2008; Phillips, 2008) .

In Western nations privacy is recognized as a basic human right – the "right to be let alone," as invented by Warren and Brandeis' (1890) *Harvard Law Review* article. It is rumored that Warren was inspired to write this article following some unfavorable news coverage of society parties his wife had given (Geuss, 2001). Therein lies the root of our contemporary understanding of privacy, connected from its inception to the intersection of public and private occupied by the media. Since then, US and European courts have defined privacy rights as citizens' entitlement to control information about themselves, and to take steps to protect personal information. For example, telephone companies are required to obtain customer permission to use or disclose personal information collected while providing services (Title 47 of the US Code of Federal Regulations, section 64.2005), illegally intercepted electronic communications may not be disclosed (Title 18, section 2511 of the US code), and unauthorized access to user files online is prohibited (US Electronic Communications Privacy Act of 1986). These stipulations present a direct recognition of the vulnerability of personal information in post-industrial democracies. Still, from a legal perspective, they do not cover the entirety of personal information that may be gathered by the commercial sector.

European Union member countries abide by stricter regulations that protect consumer privacy, specified by the Directive on Data Protection of 1998. This privacy directive safeguards individual control over consumer data and requires that foreign trading partners adhere to the same level of equal protection (Lee, 2000). While the transmission of personal information from EU member countries to outside countries without adequate privacy protection is prohibited, the nature of globalized business is such that it is possible for the EU to contractually agree to conduct business with global companies despite differences in privacy approaches (e.g. Lee, 2000). Unless these agreements prioritize personal privacy over legal protection, it is impossible to avoid potential misuses of data.

Cyberlaw efforts are typically spearheaded through the public sector, represented by non-profit organizations and centers affiliated with educational institutions. Lessig (1999) finds that in the present data-mining and monitoring environment, the responsibility to establish privacy boundaries lies with the monitored individual. The ongoing accumulation of data which transform a consumer's life into an ever-expanding record of transactions only aggravates the problem, forcing the individual to simultaneously become more cognizant of privacy boundaries and information-literate enough to set up and protect these boundaries. Legislation is formulated on this basis, requiring that individuals take the initiative in ensuring that personal information remains private. The US Financial Modernization Act (Gramm–Leach–Bliley Act of 1999) specifies that financial institutions must inform customers about their privacy practices, even though the law provides limited control to consumers regarding the use and distribution of personal data. Recently, President Obama criticized the Act as responsible for leading to subsequent deregulation and to the 2007 subprime mortgage financial crisis, and several leading economists articulated similar arguments (Krugman, 2008; Paletta and Scannel, 2009). Individuals are granted some privacy protection but must still proactively make certain that their personal information is not made available to third parties. Children understandably receive greater protection under the US Children's Online Privacy Protection Act (COPPA), which lays out specific regulations for companies targeting individuals under the age of 13. Aside from COPPA, regulatory policy in the USA is founded upon the assumption that web operators should disclose, but not adjust or restrict, information gathering and use practices.

Viewed from the public/private binary, this presents a trespass on private territory that occurs as the personal sphere and the economy intersect. Private-sector commercial imperatives, having commodified aspects of the public life, which may have brought on a demise of the public sphere (e.g., Calhoun, 1997; Habermas, 1962/1989, 1991), further appropriate personal activities of the private domain. Examples of this abound in product and media consumption, as individuals in public and private spheres function as audiences, consumers, and citizens concurrently. Through domestic routines of media consumption, audiences produce meaning that is privately and publicly relevant, as it connects processes of personal consumption to the logics of aggregate and personalized marketing (Jhally, 1990). In an environment of digitally enabled domesticity, the economic productivity of audiences is augmented, as they are not only "watched," but the labor produced by their being watched is further repurposed into mediated content re-broadcast into an audience in an ongoing loop of consumption-driven domestic productivity (Andrejevic, 2004). These are consequences of the privatization of public space, which drive several previously public activities to the non-commercialized domain of the private. As private domains become increasingly commercialized, including the private individual him/herself whose personal information may be traded in exchange for goods and services, privacy boundaries are re-negotiated.

As a result, criteria previously employed to delineate between public and private are redefined. Where it was meaningful in the past to understand the private as impenetrable to the public eye and devoted to individual pursuits, surveillance and data-mining technology leave few areas of private life that are not potentially exposed to public entities and commodifiable. Online media further render our conventional understandings of public and private anachronistic, and public and private are constantly negotiated and modified in online interactions with commercial entities. The absence of a regulatory framework dedicated to the protection of online privacy further exposes individual privacy and renders it elusive to most online users. Companies such as Microsoft Passport Services have exploited consumer information, and were pressured into revising their privacy policies and statements following a series of articles originating from Salon.com (www. salon.com). Both Yahoo! and Microsoft e-mail services reportedly divulged customer information in opposition to their stated privacy policies of not sharing personally identifiable information (Gillis, 2002). In February 2009, in response to user criticism about potential privacy violations, Facebook was forced to suspend its newly revised terms of service. Google privacy practices do not meet EU privacy standards and have been similarly criticized by several US policymakers (Bartz, 2008). Surveys reveal that consumer trust is a vital issue for web users who, although concerned about online privacy violations, still disclose personally identifiable and non-identifiable information online (Fox, 2000; Fox & Lewis, 2001). The prevalence of self-regulation forces individuals to enter a bargaining game wherein the right to be left alone is negotiated and privacy boundaries are redefined.

Privacy as luxury commodity

Companies employ privacy and terms of use statements to outline how personal information provided will be used, so that in the event of user complaints, companies are absolved of responsibility. In this manner, personal information is commercialized into the public realm, with little input from the individual in the process. It is possible for policymakers to address both individual and private-sector concerns by restricting data collection techniques (Reilly, 1999). However, as the value of online retailers increases for consumers with the disclosure of additional personal information, blocking personal information or refusing it to a retailer frequently renders a website useless to the consumer. Thus, individuals assume the risk in exchanging personal information in return for convenience and access, even though fair practice necessitates that the cost of information relinquished balances the value of the service offered (Elgesem, 1996). On the other hand, complete opt-in privacy control would lead to increased operational costs for the private sector, and restrict profits from being able to compartmentalize, re-purpose, and re-sell personal information (e.g., Farah & Higby 2001; McKenna, 2001).

Thus, privacy defined as the right to be left alone attains the characteristics of a luxury commodity, in that: (a) it becomes a good inaccessible, and disproportionately costly, to the average individual's ability to acquire and retain it; and (b) it becomes associated with social benefits inversely, in that the social cost of not forsaking parts of one's privacy in exchange for information goods and services (e-mail account free-of-charge, online social networking) places one at a disadvantage. In this manner, the right to be left alone, identified with private space, becomes a commodity bartered for the provision of goods and services associated with everyday life in an information society. This does not imply that private life ceases to exist, but the conditions under which privacy may be claimed and enjoyed are now different. For individuals, these conditions aggravate conflict between consumer behaviors and civic roles, requiring individuals to constantly and personally redefine where public ends and private begins (and vice versa) in their everyday lives. Privacy, as we have known it, becomes a property of the past, as it ceases to be a good collectively defined, but is rather a property personally delineated, negotiated, or surrendered.

A trichotomy: the social

In late modern democracies, the distinction between public and private is challenged as public life is relegated to the private territory of the domestic sphere, and the private domain is reshaped as the turf of home entertainment and commerce. As elusive and potentially misleading (Wolfe, 1997) as this distinction between private and public may be, it is nonetheless necessary in understanding how past trajectories of public and private behaviors have evolved into present-day civic obligations. A discussion of the public and private binary becomes meaningful then not as a means for further polarizing theory and practice, but rather as a way of appreciating the tensions forming between these two boundaries. Human behaviors unfold over and require both public and private domains of thought and action, but become confined in situations where the public overwhelms the private; conversely, the private overpowers the public. Thus, political thought has critiqued economic and socio-cultural conditions that have allowed the private to swallow up the public and have simultaneously cut off the home from the public realm (e.g., Arendt, 1958, 1970; Calhoun, 1992; Habermas, 1962/1989, 1992; Lasch, 1979; Sennett, 1974). As late modern democracies fully absorb the decline of economic systems that emphasized public over private (communism) and accept economic systems that prioritize private over public as the only alternative (capitalism), it becomes essential to understand how employing analytical binaries may subsequently produce seemingly unavoidable dualisms.

To lead lives that are entirely private or entirely public is an impossibility and runs counter to human nature. Preserving the boundaries of public and private permits the leading of lives that may be simultaneously spontaneous and deliberative, personal and political. As Elshtain (1997) suggests, a "richly complex private sphere requires some freedom from all-encompassing public imperatives to survive," and, conversely, the "public world itself must nurture . . . a commitment to preserve, protect, and defend human beings in their capacities as private persons, *as well as* to encourage and enable men and women alike to partake in the practical activity of politics" (p. 180). It is the balance between public responsibilities to the polity and private attention to the nourishment of the self that enables public and private to exist in a parallel and converging manner, allowing the imperatives of the private world to turn into synergy in the public world, and the collectivity of the public world to inspire private thought, reflection, and action.

The private domain becomes disruptive to the extent that it transforms the right to privacy into privatism, as, in Arendt's (1958) words, "To live an entirely public life means above all to be deprived of all things essential to a truly human life" (p. 54). Likewise, the public realm transforms into an apparatus of ideological suppression as it collects privatized self-interest that never materializes into collective interest. For Arendt (1958), this delicate balance between private and public is complicated by the rise of the *social*, as the realm where private interests attain public import, not through processes of collectivity, but rather, as brought on by the rise of the nation-state and the conditions of industrial economy. These conditions forsake the division between public and private for the economic organization of multiple economic family units into a single "super-human family," termed society (Arendt, 1958, p. 40). The *social* exists as an alternative to the bipolar continuum of public and private; however, it is possible for the social to sustain elements of both public and private practices without being subsumed by either. Ideas of a civil or cosmopolitan society are thus structured upon the trichotomy postulated by the *private*, the *public*, and the *social*.

Wolfe (1997) formulates this trichotomy in the following manner, distinguishing between (a) "a *private* sector in which we appropriately judge behavior by whether it maximizes individual freedom or self-interest," (b) "a *public* sector in which we make decisions that are meant to apply equally to everyone in the society (even as we recognize the near impossibility of doing this)," and (c) "a realm of distinct publics" (p. 196). It is in the realm of these distinct publics, or Arendt's socio-economic units that comprise a super-human family, that the *social* takes shape. These publics are partially collective, in that they share norms and common goals, but the basis of this collectivity is social, not political. They are also partially private, in that they may shield the individual from the public realm in ways that enable the development of self-interest and private identity. The fundamental difference here, however, is that the motivation behind action (or inaction) is social, and determined by the semi-private and semi-public social needs of these multiple *private publics* that formulate the social.

The *social* gains relevance in late modern democracies as it collapses tropes of achieving individual and collective autonomy into a combined sphere of activity that is socially motivated, but employs public and private boundaries that are fluid and constantly renegotiated. Within this fluid context, the economic, social, political, cultural, or legal origin of thoughts and action is frequently confused with the economic, social, political, or legal texture of the consequence, as it becomes impossible, and ultimately meaningless, to classify human activities in absolute categories. Conditions of technological convergence merely augment and intensify these themes, as they provide the fluid architectural landscape in which the social is reified and thrives. The ways in which individuals internalize the convergence of public and private, operate in the social, and absorb technological convergence as audiences, publics, and citizens are explored in the next two chapters.

3

Converged Media, Converged
Audiences, and Converged Publics

Human activity traverses planes that are private, public, and social, not necessarily in that order or in exclusivity. The architecture of these spaces informs human action by suggesting, concealing, or disrupting activities, "organizing," in Michel de Certeau's (1984) words, "an ensemble of possibilities and interdictions . . . while the walker actualizes some of these possibilities" (p. 98). Online digital media contribute to the architecture of contemporary civic spaces around which public, private, and social activity develops, by suggesting possibilities for interaction. These are often understood as the inherent affordances of technologies, that is, intrinsic potentialities which suggest that it is "easier to use them for some purposes than for others" (Buckingham, 2008, p. 12). The technological architecture within which affordances are presented supplies individuals with a collage of choices, further multiplied, adapted, or restricted by human action and reaction. A combination of infrastructure, content, design, and technological architecture refers to the simulation of physicality that virtual environments present individuals with. Technological architecture, like all architecture, is social.

Technology construed as simple cause or consequence of human action becomes the deterministic and linear driving force or result of human action. In contrast, technology as architecture is integrated to the rhythms of everyday life, presenting the environment within which individual thought takes the form of action. As an amalgamation of technical, social, human, and historical circumstances, technologies carry the stamp of the era within which they came to be (Hutchby, 2001). In this context, the communicative affordances of technology are seamlessly negotiated among individuals, society, and the technology itself, producing technology that is both "socially shaped and socially shaping" (Buckingham, 2008, p. 12; Williams, 1974). A flexible architecture is cognizant of these affordances, yet permissive of the dialectic process between humans and technology.

This chapter is about what is unique in online media, and how this leads to a singular contribution to contemporary democracies. When asked to identify unique attributes of emerging online technologies, words like interactivity, anonymity, convergence, hyper-reality, community, and identity come to mind. All of these characteristics lead to unique uses of online media, but the one that complicates matters when we seek to evaluate the democratic merit of online media is convergence. Media scholars and producers are accustomed to discussing the convergence of media content, focusing on the overlap and combination of multimedia content that new media enable. For media industry people, media convergence carries significant consequences for the economic and organizational convergence of media organizations. The focus here is on the architectural environment technological convergence presents for democratic practices. The architectural environment constructed by convergent technologies accentuates affordances of a confluent or networked nature. Thus, in the democratic sphere of interaction, convergence simultaneously melds *and* blurs traditional boundaries among media, and among audiences of different media (print/TV/online/radio), audiences and publics, citizens and consumers, consumers and producers.

The contemporary citizen frequently engages in multiple media use, which may produce variable amounts of social capital, and the democratic impact of which cannot be measured readily. Concurrently, online media which enable acts of civic engagement frequently carry a distinct commercial component, which confuses the roles of citizen and consumer. The individual frequently combines the use of several media, rarely sitting down to just read the newspaper, just listen to the news on the radio, only watch TV or participate in online political discussion groups, thus routinely functioning as a multitasking consumer/producer of multimedia. These concurrent and overlapping uses are typically integrated or domesticated into everyday communicative routines that form networked social landscapes (Bakardjieva & Smith, 2001; Baym, Zhang & Lin, 2004; Humphreys, 2005). At the same time, the individual is hailed as audience member, citizen, consumer, and content producer by a variety of interest groups, public and private, that seek to maximize access to the individual's economic productivity by tapping into the converged media potential (e.g., Bauman, 2005; Bird, 2003; Deuze, 2007; Ettema & Whitney, 1994; Hartley, 2005; Hay, Grossberg & Wartella, 1996; Jenkins, 2006a & b; Silverstone, 2007; Silverstone & Hirsch, 1992). Converged media architecture presents a menu of converged media practices, which converged media audiences and converged media publics employ, expand, or reject, so that the circle of convergence in everyday life resumes its infinite course.

Convergence in everyday life

It is impossible to define convergence without situating it first within the historical context it has emerged out of. While convergence as a term refers to the confluence of a variety of technologies, it is essential to establish that: (a) convergence is not a defining characteristic of all technology, and (b) convergence does not present a characteristic exclusive to technology. With this in mind, information processing technologies are characterized by a confluence of services and platforms, more so than other past, or contemporary, media or technologies. At the same time, the convergence of information technologies is rooted in a greater convergence of social, cultural, political, and economic tendencies which enable and are enabled by technological convergence. Therefore, the conflux of a variety of technologies is neither a mystical attribute of the technologies themselves, nor solely a consequence of socio-cultural, economic, and political development driven by humans. Convergence refers to trends and practices within *and* beyond technology, which describe how individuals connect with their everyday environments through habits of social, political, economic, and cultural texture.

Even though convergence has become a popularized term, its

origins lie in socio-economic patterns associated with the emergence of the information society or the gradual transition into a mode of existence that is decidedly post-industrial. Bell (1981) had identified the present post-industrial state as the information society, which is marked by: (a) a change from a goods-producing to a service society, (b) the centrality of the codification of theoretical knowledge for innovation in technology, and (c) the creation of a new "intellectual technology" as a key tool of systems analysis and decision theory (p. 501). In this society, information and knowledge are the key variables, much like labor and capital were the primary components of industrial society, wherein they drive an economic organization of a formation that capitalizes on the confluence of the political, social, and cultural. While several disagree that the patterns described are new or unique (Schiller, 2000) and several identify them as typical of latter-stage or information-driven capitalism (Schement & Curtis, 1997; Schement & Lievrouw, 1987), all recognize that the fluidity of information as a commodity places social, economic, political, and cultural transactions on a plane that is networked and interconnected. The effect of overlapping confluent networks has been described by some as a network or information society (Castells, 2000; van Dijk, 1999; Webster, 2006), the wealth of interconnected and confounded networks (Benkler, 2006), or emblematic of convergence (Jenkins, 2006a & b). The origin of this networked effect is part economic (e.g., Machlup, 1962; Schiller, 2000; Schement & Curtis, 1997; Schement & Lievrouw, 1987), part technological (Bell, 1981; Kling, 1996; Negroponte, 1998; Rheingold, 1993), and always sensitive to socio-cultural context (Castells, 2000; Webster, 2006). Rather than delving into a discussion of whether it is socio-economic convergence that drives technological convergence or the other way around, it might be more meaningful to situate these phenomena in their historical context.

First, information technologies possess the capacity for combining and providing access to various and diverse goods and services. This capability rests on the fluidity of information as a product and the interconnectedness of the technologies upon which information travels. While the origins of the information technologies that enable convergence can be traced to the information revolution of the late seventies (Bell, 1981), and information trading emerges as a prevalent aspect of the gross national product in the late fifties and sixties (Machlup, 1962), convergent technologies begin to truly dominate market and social logic in the nineties (Benkler, 2006; Castells, 2000; Shapiro & Varian, 1998).

Second, convergent information technologies are both the product and driving force of capitalist infrastructures, simultaneously reinforcing and repurposing capitalist modes of production and consumption. Castells (2000) described this reciprocal trend by noting that "the information technology revolution has been instrumental in . . . restructuring . . . the capitalist system from the 1980s onwards," while, at the same time, "this technological revolution was itself shaped . . . by the logic and interests of advanced capitalism, without being reducible to the expression of such interests" (p. 13). The effects of this reciprocity are variant, based on the history, culture, and institutions of each unique society and its specific relationship to global capitalism and information technology.

Third, regardless of the reciprocity of influence, the dominant economic system of capitalism prioritizes the commodification of information. The profit motive provides the incentive to turn information not into a free-for-all, but into a commodity to be traded. The use of information technologies is an attempt to control and manage the industrial growth spurred by the industrial revolution, and sustained by the post-industrial state of being. Convergent technologies, regardless of how democratizing, social, or innovative they may be, are rooted in the logic of commodification. While commodification does not preclude non-commercial uses of information technologies, it is also not inherently suggestive of them. Thus, the tendency in advanced capitalist societies to promote the commercial side of convergence must be taken under consideration when interpreting the multi-layered impact of information technologies on societies. During the early ARPANET (Advanced Research Projects Agency Network) days, this led to a perception of the Internet as a venture too risky for private sector telecommunications companies, leading to government and education assuming a leading role in the development of Internet infrastructure. The traditional capitalist economic infrastructure possessed no way of supporting innovative and convergent technological applications until the arrival of venture capital as a way of using private equity to finance early-stage, high-potential, high-risk, and high-growth companies. The growth of venture capital as an investment strategy is associated with the financing of Silicon Valley start-up companies in the seventies, and to this day presents the dominant mode of embracing technologically convergent ventures within a capitalist infrastructure, rendering them a sub-species of industrial capitalism. Thus, the economic potential of convergent technologies is prioritized, and the socio-cultural aspect of technologies becomes relevant as long as it is integrated in a profitable manner, frequently leading into socio-cultural uses characterized by superficiality (e.g., Sennett, 2006).

And yet, there is a way for modified models of capitalism to embrace the socio-cultural aspect of technology without commercializing interaction. Social and economic imperatives need not operate in mutual exclusivity, and convergent technologies suggest meaningful ways for the humanization of capitalist infrastructures. It is within this context that scholars will engage the concept of convergence, as an element of the newer paradigm of an increasingly networked economy and society. Castells (2000) understands network societies as the product of the following interrelated characteristics: (a) technologies that act on information, as opposed to information to act on technology; (b) a pervasiveness of new technology effects; (c) the networking logic behind the systems driving information technologies; (d) flexibility; and (e) the convergence of technologies into a highly integrated system (pp. 70–1). The interactions of a network society, whether of economic, socio-cultural, political, or combined origin, take place within a networked spatial terrain that enables synchronicity and elasticity in communication without physical proximity, which Castells (2000) terms the *space of flows*.

Convergence enables but also takes shape within the space of flows, and is understood as the outcome of the growing interdependence of networked technologies as well as the driving force behind them. The intellectual origins of convergence can be

traced back to the work of several scholars who described processes related to convergence or conditions necessary to achieve
it. Heidegger (1954/1977), in *The Question Concerning Technology*,
returned to the Greek origin and Ancient Greek definition of technology (τεχνολογία) to locate the connection between technology
and doing, or, in Heidegger's terms, *bringing forth (ποίησις)*. The
Greeks used the term *technology* to describe all activities associated
with the invention and employment of, and deliberation about,
technology, which was used to refer both to applied activities and
skills and to the arts of the mind and the fine arts. The tendency
to use the term to refer to technologies that are applied or deliver
is associated with industrial-era technological innovations that
radically transformed transportation and communication. At its
original inception, however, the root of the term *technology* derived
from the word *techne (τέχνη)*, associated with poetry and forms of
artistic expression dedicated to ontological pursuits. These forms
of artistic expression are in equal parts applied and abstract, and
make no distinction between those who produce and those who
consume a technology. From this point of view, Heidegger argued
that modern technology *enframes* human existence, thus enabling
humans to gather up the environment that makes up their existence, and through this experience arrive at a fuller understanding
of what it means *to be.*

In modern societies then, it is not uncommon to ascribe to technology a function centrifugal or centripetal to the human existence,
which could potentially advance individuals' ability to make sense
of their own environments. Toffler (1980), in describing the Third
Wave and the transition from an industrial to a post-industrial or
information society, emphasized the presence of knowledge-based
production, fluid organizations and subcultures, mass customization and personalization, all enabled by technologies that are jointly
configured. Toffler's *prosumers* emerged out of this environment,
describing individuals who employ technologies to seamlessly
flow from consumption to production of content and vice versa.
The intellectual ancestry of the term *convergence* can be traced to
Ithiel de Sola Pool, whose *Technologies of Freedom* described the
media processes leading to a convergence of production modes,

and who is recognized by several as the prophet of convergence (e.g., Jenkins, 2006a). De Sola Pool (1983) defined convergence as a process "blurring the lines between media," allowing a "single physical means – be it wires, cables, or airwaves – [to] carry services that in the past were provided in separate ways. Conversely, a service that was provided in the past by any medium . . . can now be provided in several different physical ways" (p. 23). Through this process, the exclusive one-to-one relationship that existed between a medium and its use is challenged. Consequently, the linear communication connecting media producer via transmitted message to potential media consumer is upset.

From this point on, de Certeau (1984) further redefined the distinction between producer and consumer, as he understood consumption to be a form of production that occurs when the individual becomes "dislodged" from the product (p. 31). In the everyday activities of production through consumption that ensue, characterized by routine, poaching, fragmentation, and "tireless but quiet activity," de Certeau set the stage for the quiet producer or consumer to function (p. 31). Toffler's *prosumers* ultimately engaged technology from a more active state than the one de Certeau described in the ruses of everyday production/ consumption. For de Certeau, the convergence of production and consumption lies in poaching, which de Certeau defines as the consumer's way of seizing control of and re-appropriating manufactured content. Variable forms of cultural poaching allow media consumers to insert new layers of meaning into already-produced content, thus producing meaning while consuming content. It is textual poaching that lays the foundation for a participatory culture of consumption within which convergent uses of technology are practiced (Jenkins, 1992).

Of course, for information technologies, it is the fluidity and interconnectedness of overlapping capabilities that allow multiple networked planes of activity to form and host participatory and multimedia acts of consumption/production. As Manovich (2001, 2005) argues, convergent media possess both *remixed* and *remixable* properties, opening them up to the influence of existent societal structures and of independent socio-cultural actors.

Within the context of a networked society, then, convergence can be defined as the confluence of "specific technologies into a highly integrated system, within which old, separate technological trajectories become literally indistinguishable" (Castells, 2000, p. 72). Thus, on a primary level, convergence implies the combined and overlapping production and distribution of technologies, which permit the production, transmission, and consumption of content across a variety of multimedia formats that collapse into a single content feed only to disperse into multiple and global points of contact. Technologies that were previously separated are now produced and made available synergistically, ranging from chips that embed a variety of data, to communication networks that transmit multi-mediated content, to machines that serve a variety of overlapping functions, to content that is deliverable as easily through television as it is via mobile technology. Technological convergence is an ever-evolving process, enabled by information technologies that develop knowledge by acting on the basis of previously existing and presently produced knowledge.

Yet, isolating convergence to the technological realm underplays the historical circumstances that have shaped and are shaped by the process of convergence. As a cultural process, convergence implies a dialogue between flexible, evolving, and interconnected modes of media production and individuals who seamlessly flow through media platforms with little conscious regard for conventional producer/consumer binaries. From this viewpoint, Jenkins (2006a) defines convergence broadly as:

> A word that describes technological, industrial, cultural and social changes in the ways media circulate within our culture. Some common ideas referenced by the term include the flow of content across multiple media platforms, the cooperation between multiple media industries, the search for new structures of media financing that fall at the interstices between old and new media, and the migratory behavior of media audiences who would go almost anywhere in search of the kind of entertainment experiences they want. Perhaps most broadly, media convergence refers to a situation in which multiple media systems coexist and where media content flows fluidly across them. Convergence is understood here as an ongoing process or series of intersections between different media systems not a fixed relationship. (p. 282)

It becomes evident that convergence expresses the fluidity, inter-connectedness, and information-centrism of post-industrial societies. However, as a cultural process, it embodies elements of technological *and socio-cultural* evolution, adaptation, and re-appropriation of previous modes of co-existence. As Deuze (2007) specifies, "This convergence is not just a technological process," and it must therefore also be recognized as "having a cultural logic of its own, blurring the lines between production and consumption, between making media and using media, and between active or passive spectatorship of mediated culture" (p. 74).

Convergence synopsizes change of a gradual nature. The consequences of convergence are not instantly inflicted nor are they equally experienced by all media and all audiences. Moreover, as convergences embodies a variety of both abstract and applied practices, spanning and blending the spheres of media production, the economy, politics, and socio-cultural activities, it is not uncommon for the term to change semantically, depending on the context in which it is used. For instance, Jenkins (2006a) has defined corporate convergence as "the commercially directed flow of media content" (p. 282). Hartley (2005) employed the term *creative industries* to describe the "conceptual and practical convergence of the creative arts (individual talent) with cultural industries (mass scale), in the context of new media technologies (ICTs) within a new knowledge economy, for the use of newly interactive citizen-consumers" (p. 5).

The context of this volume is that of civic engagement in a digital age, and thus the concept of convergence is explicated as a means of interpreting the democratizing affordances of information communication technologies. In the political sphere, convergence of public and private, as argued in the previous chapter, signifies the collapse of economic, social, political, cultural, or legal textures into a single converged landscape of activity that fluidly traverses public and private with little desire for permanent affiliation to either. Individuals appreciate the widespread and permeating impact of the convergence and acknowledge that societal institutions have trouble keeping up with the pace of convergence (Anderson & Rainie, 2006; Fox, Anderson, & Rainie, 2005). In the next few sections, I examine how the potentialities of convergent technologies contribute to the architecture of publicly private and privately public spaces around which civic activity develops. Conditions of technological convergence can be understood as relevant to: (a) the means through which individuals become civically engaged (*convergence of technologies*); (b) the physical and imagined spaces on which civic intention is enacted (*convergence of spaces*); and (c) the continuum of activities that shape and are shaped by a converged technological architecture (*convergence of practices*). It is along these three themes that convergence, in the context of civic engagement, is explicated.

Convergence of technologies

Technological convergence refers to the interconnectedness afforded through networked capabilities of information technologies and is relevant to various levels of interaction involving individuals, organizations, businesses, groups, and greater societal configurations. It is therefore reasonable to explicate technological convergence along the three dimensions of micro, meso, and macro levels, all of which lend evidence of the same phenomena of interconnectedness in progress. Within the context of the information society, Schement and Curtis (1997) have employed micro-meso-macro-level analysis to synthesize findings on the diffusion of interconnectedness through multiple converged spheres of interaction. Convergent technologies present the means through which the interconnectedness of the information society is made available to individuals for personal use, and thus are experienced variably on micro, meso, and macro levels of interaction.

At the micro level, individuals experience convergence in their social relations with families, circles of friends, and acquaintances. Uses of technologies become indicative of variable individual needs to optimize social contact, manage time, and express identity in ways that combine a variety of communication channels. Research is affirmative of the social capability of converged technologies (e.g., Baym, 1995, 1997; Jones, 1997a & b, 1998; Rheingold, 1993; Walther, 1995, 1996), their potential for identity expression and self-presentation (e.g., Bolter, 1996; Haraway, 1991; Turkle, 1984,

1995, 1996, 1997), and the ways in which they enhance, complement, or substitute for other forms of communication (Howard & Jones, 2004; Katz & Rice, 2002; Kraut et al., 1998, 2002; LaRose, Eastin, & Gregg, 2001; Papacharissi, 2000, 2002a & b). The same researchers recognize the occasionally fragmented texture of communities sustained through converged technologies, the narcissistically motivated nature of self-expression fostered online, and the convergence of networks of social contact that require both offline and online channels of communication for development and sustenance.

This does not necessarily imply that the number of relationships increases for everyone while the felt intensity of those relationships decreases. Rather, given that this is an affordance of technologies, this suggests that it becomes easier for individuals to use converged technologies to broaden the perimeter of their social activity and to supplement the strength of bonds to fellow human beings. Individuals select from a plateau of communicative possibilities, some of which are converged, to mix, match, and substitute channels, the efficiency of which is subjectively determined and constantly re-evaluated, based on the evolving individual daily routines.

Recent research affirms the ability of convergent technologies to simultaneously expand the scope and modify the depth of networks of social relations (e.g., Haythornthwaite, 2005; Haythornthwaite & Wellman, 1998; Haythornthwaite, Wellman, & Mantei, 1995). Online interaction frequently complements or serves as an alternative to face-to-face interaction (Wellman, Haase, Witte, & Hampton, 2001), in ways that have positive effects on social capital (Hampton & Wellman, 2003). Multimedia platforms that facilitate the convergence of offline and online spheres of social contact, like Facebook, LinkedIn, MySpace, and other social network sites (SNSs) facilitate the cultivation of strong ties to friends and families and the expansion of weaker ties to widely dispersed spheres of acquaintances (boyd, 2004, 2006; boyd & Ellison, 2007; Ellison, Steinfield, & Lampe, 2007). At the same time, they promote a commonly shared protocol of conduct structured around symbolic use of text and images, manipulated to convey sociability, complexity of involvement, and emotion through self-expression (Donath, 2007; Donath & Boyd, 2004). Moreover, online networks of friends may be employed to cultivate carefully controlled impressions of the self (Dominick, 1999; Donath, 1998; Papacharissi, 2002a & b), performances structured around class affiliation (Papacharissi, 2009) and cultures of taste (Liu, 2007; Liu, Maes, & Davenport, 2006).

At the micro level then, the individual's sphere of social contact is activated and sustained through both older and newer media for communication that operate jointly or that the individual independently chooses to combine. The result is a sphere of social contact that is more fluid but may also appear fragmented and contain elements of superficiality. The individual is able to manipulate converged technologies to enhance the substance and depth of this fluid social sphere, but this becomes a function of individual agency and the potentiality of the technologies at hand. The private sphere of the home, from which most operations of a social nature emanate, becomes fluid and mobile, enabling the individual to simulate the private domesticity of the home in physical locations extraneous to it: the workplace, public spaces, the mobile sphere. Thus, the rhetoric of the converged home borrows from the implied fluidity and transience of hotel spaces, which are structured to accommodate fleeting presence and structured stability to a lesser extent.

At the meso level, organizations experience convergence in their modes of information processing and content production, which then modify the ways in which they relate to each other as well as potential audiences and consumers. For organizations and media systems, convergence is experienced across ownership, production, and distribution of content. Vertical *and* horizontal models of ownership optimize cost efficiency and interconnectedness, thus combining organizations that are organically connected (e.g., a variety of media organizations) to external organizational entities that do not share inherent connections (e.g., ownership of NBC by General Electric). Combined ownership of a variety of product platforms (film, news, TV, magazine, print, gaming, online platforms, music, electronics, consumer goods, home appliances, and a variety of other products) lends itself to countless possibilities of converged advertising and marketing.

In terms of converged production, companies have been able to maximize cost efficiency and speed of content production through newer media technologies while at the same time combining their productive resources into highly concentrated monopolies or oligopolies of media content. The result is a diversification of production *platforms* but a centralization of the production *process*, potentially leading to formulaic productions of content. Jenkins (2006a) points to global reality hit *American Idol* as one such illustration of a cross-promotional globalized marketing apparatus for a variety of associated media and non-media products, all circulated through the converged context of reality TV and centrally administered by the organization entity owning the show and collateral ventures.

Finally, distribution channels or delivery technologies attain a transient nature as they emerge, converge, transmit, and become obsolete depending on the evolution of the converged media they are borne out of (Deuze, 2007; Jenkins, 2006a). Thus, the medium (newspaper) remains the same, but the platform upon which it is delivered is constantly re-defined by historically sensitive technical developments, including paper, print, online news portal, blog, and other formats. This process does not necessarily guarantee that all media or delivery modes will become obsolete. Rather, through a process of *remediation*, newer media achieve cultural singularity by mimicking, rivaling, and ultimately refashioning earlier media as they fashion a unique identity of their own (Bolter & Brusin, 2000). This becomes apparent through remediations of earlier media, including the remediation of painting by photography, stage production and photography by film, and film, vaudeville and radio by television. Both newer and earlier media possess singularity, although this singularity is frequently re-considered, revised, and remediated with the arrival of additional innovation.

These developments are absorbed by the audience landscape as the way in which audiences and consumers associate with media organizations, channels, and content is also remediated. On a primary level, converged technologies permit media content to become more open and readily manipulable for audiences that were previously accustomed to a closed-ended structure. This potentiality promotes the cultivation of a participatory culture among media audiences, thus inserting a bottom-up consumer-driven element to the traditionally bottom-down process of creating media content. Thus, convergence is afforded by communicative technologies, but is acted out only to the extent that audiences participate in the collective production of media content. As Jenkins (2006a) clarifies, "[convergence] does not occur through media appliances . . . it occurs within the brains of individual consumers and through their social interactions with others" (p. 3). Thus, while convergence allows several individuals to function as both *producer* and *consumer*, or *produsers* of mediated content, *produsing* ability and activity is neither constant nor static. Individuals possess the potential to flow through various stages of involvement with media content, and convergence presents such a stage, experienced on a variety of different levels by different users.

To the extent that participatory media culture becomes collective and critically diffused, then it could present an alternative to media power. Perhaps convergence is experienced in a more potent manner internally, as individuals who produce meaning via practices of consumption then transition to a state of producing content, to then further advance to a stage where they seamlessly consume, produce meaning, and possibly produce content without acknowledging a real difference between the two activities. For many, the ability to consume and produce content has transferred media labor to audiences who are essentially working for the media, by producing i-reports, tele-voting reality stars, forming niche target groups out of their lifestyle habits and accidentally or intentionally producing content to be further exploited by mainstream media. Lured by the guise of participatory media and the promise of power over broadcast content, audiences of producers contribute to programming presented as open, never to be compensated for this labor (Andrejevic, 2003; Deuze, 2007).

Finally, at the macro level, convergence is experienced globally and locally in the form of longer-lasting developments that modify the economic, socio-cultural, and political structures that harbor human activity. Hartley (2005) describes the most potent of these transitions as occurring within the frame of *creative industries*, that is, the culture industries served by technologies of convergence. On the macro level, convergence is absorbed by creative industries, copyright industries, content industries, cultural industries, and digital content (Hartley, 2005).

Creative industries are characterized by the work of creative individuals and are located in the realm of the arts, including film, music, publishing, interactive software, advertising, architecture, and design. Copyright industries are located in the same realm, but are defined by the commercial viability of creative industry output, reflected in the convergent tendencies of open source software, Creative Commons licensing, and market attempts to integrate convergent products (Canclini, 2005; Lessig, 2005; Meikle, 2005). Content industries are characterized by the type of creative output industries generate. Cultural industries are sensitive to public funding and public policymaking, as reflected by attempts of commercial cultural industry, like Hollywood, to integrate converged products (Miller, Govil, McMurria, & Maxwell, 2005). Digital content is shaped by the combination of technology and the locus of industry production, and is represented by alternative convergent incarnations of *webisodes*, online access to digital content, and, in general, content-producing processes that are open and in progress (Eco, 2005; Maramotti, 2005; Murray, 2005; Roscoe, 2005). Hartley (2005) conceptualizes these as forming a value-chain pyramid, in which value is allocated from top to bottom, beginning with cultural industries resting above the creative industries, which are both situated above the distribution industries. Copyright industries are born as a function of the pyramid constructed and operate externally, connecting creative content to the industries and to external entities.

Creative industries are meaningful in understanding the ways in which convergence infiltrates the production of culture on an international level, infusing it with elements of collectivity, openness, and interconnectedness. As such, the concept of creative industries permits the explication of technological convergence as a fundamental characteristic of information societies. Naturally there are economic, political, and legal consequences to global patterns of interconnectedness, but creative industries underline the structures across which converged content is created, transferred, and remediated. Some of these structures carry a commercial component (copyright industries), others are politically influenced (cultural industries), while yet others are socio-culturally driven (digital content, content industries). The creative industries structure is reflective of the cultural logic behind the organization of industries employing some aspect of convergent technologies. The economic logic of creative industries presents a negotiation between convergent tendencies and economic tensions, posed by the monopolistic and profit-driven structure of most commercial media organizations (Bagdikian, 2004; McChesney, 2004, 2008). Media content, produced by commercial media, presents a commodity targeted to specific audiences. The ability to produce on a technologically converged infrastructure enables media industries to target multiple audiences and deliver content through a plurality of convergent and cross-referencing formats, but it does not remove the profit motive from the economic structure of the commercial media institutions in late modern capitalist societies. Thus, convergence expands and contributes variables, but also expands the economic foundation of the media marketing equation, which includes global and glocal networks (Castells, 2009).

For the individual operating within the context of global convergence tendencies, technological literacy and fluency become imperatives. As the conditions upon which creative industries are structured prevail in the media market, individuals are recruited as capable creative industry workers, often expected to exhibit know-how previously associated only with professional information workers. Thus, in the creative industry context, individuals are expected to be informed of privacy rights and able to protect them; are allotted the journalistic tasks of collecting, perusing, classifying, and frequently reporting information; and must display the savvy of seasoned legal and security officers in protecting their identity in online interactions. Hartley (2000) used the term *redactional society* to describe a society in which all individuals are afforded the task of editing or redacting information, a task previously associated with journalism as a civically charged profession. Technologically converged societies, however, require redactional skills of all their users, if they are to survive media that enable them to consume and publish across public and private planes.

Convergence of spaces

The collapse of public and private boundaries that separate spheres of work, domesticity, leisure, civic life, and other individual activity is not a phenomenon unique to information societies. The printing press changed conventions for transforming private thought into public expression. Technologies of transportation connected previously incoherent private spaces. Communication itself is a practice invented to traverse from private to public terrains of articulation. In modern societies, electronic media predispose communication by suggesting a juxtaposition of private and public boundaries that human activity advances from. Meyrowitz (1986) described this as the ability of electronic media to remove, or at least rearrange, boundaries between public and private spaces, affecting our lives not so much through content, but rather "by changing the 'situational geography' of social life" (p. 6). In the seminal *No Sense of Place*, Meyrowitz (1986), likened this potential to the architectural effect that would be created were all walls physically separating rooms, houses, offices, buildings, and all concrete structures to be lifted. The result would combine several previously distinct situations, creating a paradox: an inharmonious continuum of several disconnected conversations, simultaneously aware of but potentially discordant with each other. This confluence of public and private boundaries exposes individuals to a variety of potential audiences, some intentional and several accidental. Still, because the norms of evaluating social behavior remain the same, individuals feel compelled to adjust their behavior so that it may be compatible with a variety of different situations and audiences.

Meyrowitz (1986) wrote mostly about television, and its ability to juxtapose public and private conversations in ways that changed childhood, re-arranged private/public gender discourses, and demystified politics. Through their tendency to channel or remediate preceding media, information communication technologies further pronounce this effect. The confluence of public and private spaces is especially prevalent in net-based forms of communication. For example, bloggers voluntarily expose the privacy of diary-form introspection to multiple public audiences. YouTube videos broadcast context-free pieces of deeply idiosyncratic experiences. Online social networks combine audiences in ways that simultaneously group and segment social communication. The result is a loss of the unique connection of interaction to place. This connection serves to orient the individual and provide, in Meyrowitz's terms, a *sense of place*. The convergence of technologies connects technological platforms in a manner that potentially combines planes of interaction. Thus, previously disconnected or remote spheres of interaction are exposed to each other. This new-found proximity enables previously disconnected nodes of communication to become active. At the same time, behavioral adjustment is required, so that communication that previously operated on the premise of distance becomes accustomed to the lack of it. Still, the process of modifying behavior so as to be palatable to a variety of audiences is not new for individuals. In everyday cycles of self-presentation and impression formation, individuals perform on multiple stages, creating a "face" for each interaction and developing "faces" for a variety of situational contexts (Goffman, 1959). These performances are structured around presenting a face and are defined by Goffman as information games, revolving on "a potentially infinite cycle of concealment, discovery, false revelation, and rediscovery" (p. 13).

Information communication technologies provide individuals with additional tools for the production of more detailed and controlled performances of the self (Donath & boyd, 2004; Papacharissi, 2002a & b). Given the level of control over verbal and non-verbal cues in a variety of online contexts, individuals concoct controlled performances that "give off" precisely the intended "face" individuals planned for, something not as easily controllable in offline settings. Goffman (1959) describes this as the "setting," for the presentation of the self, that is, the "furniture, décor, physical layout and other background items which supply the scenery and stage props," with which the individuals articulate the "front," or a general introductory performance of the self, as opposed to the "backstage," where a more authentic self resides (p. 97). Thus, information communication technologies expand the *expressive equipment* at hand, possibly allowing greater control of the distance between the *front* and *backstage* areas of the self – what is presented and that which is reserved. However, what is afforded by the multimedia capabilities of information technologies is supplanted by the convergence of spaces sustained by the same media.

While it is possible for this convergence to displace the situational character of some communication, non-verbal and verbal cues afforded by technology enable the mediation of situational information. Perhaps a more apt metaphor can be located away from Meyrowitz's dramatic *collapse* of place to what Scannell (1996) has termed the *doubling of place*. Scannell explains that in late modern life, "public events . . . occur simultaneously in two different places: the place of the event itself and that in which it is watched and heard. Broadcasting mediates *between* these two sites" (p. 76). This suggestion is not far removed from Lippmann's (1922) *pseudoenvironments*, created for the convenience of relaying experiences taking place in remote locations. The difference is of course that, with electronic media, the event occurs simultaneously in both locations, creating two equally viable realities. With converged technologies, the effect is further multiplied, creating a plurality of overlapping or mutually exclusive social realities. Consequently, social relationships are multiplied, creating the potential for multiple performances of the self occurring on a variety of different stages (Moores, 2004). The multiplication of social environments and consequent pluralization of social relationships does not de facto lead to a lost sense of place, implying displaced physical location, but also displaced sense of social status. This is the reason why many perceive the "doubling" or "multiplying" metaphor a more accurate reflection of the role played by technology (e.g., Couldry, 2000, 2004; Moores, 2004; Ross, 2004; Scannell, 1996). The resulting space is a converged continuum, made up by discordant blocks of activity, or "homogeneous, yet at the same time broken into fragments" (Lefebvre, 1974/1991, p. 342).

The metaphor of multiplied space communicates an impact of convergent technologies upon space that is of quantifiable nature. Multiplied space, however fragmented, suggests the pluralization of space. As a metaphor, multiplication speaks to the quantity of space generated, but is not descriptive of the quality of space multiplied. Does multiplied space contain properties similar to the attributes of the space from which it evolved? What are the qualitative elements of multiplied space, and how do they connect, replicate, or differ from the properties of actual space? Architecture employs the technique of folding to suggest the ways in which multiplied space may be fragmented and rearranged, so as to present not just multiplied space surfaces, but surfaces that lend themselves to the creation of more flexible shapes. I argue that a similar effect is produced by convergent technologies. Space is not only multiplied, it is simultaneously fragmented and reassembled into structures that attain greater reflexivity.

Architect and academic Sophia Vyzoviti (2001, 2003) has employed the term *supersurfaces,* to describe the spatial possibilities enabled by the technique of folding. Using paper as an empirical model, she explains how flat surfaces can be transformed into volumes through cutting, weaving, twisting, winding, and further manipulating woven forms (see images 4 and 5). The resulting *supersurfaces* evolve beyond the fixity of manipulated artifacts, to suggest an appeal that lies in their lightness and flexibility. Supersurfaces are appealing because they are remixed and remix-able. Similarly, *convergent supersurfaces* describes the spatial effects of convergent technology on place. Space is disjointed, recon-nected, woven, and re-organized into places light enough to rest on the outer landscapes of greater systemic structures, and not heavy enough to dissolve into the systemic core of the institutions of democracy. The concept of convergent supersurface captures both the promise and peril of cyberspaces: flexible enough to sustain a variety of conversations, too flexible to have the weight required for a lasting impact. These spaces develop upon the outer fabrics of traditional democratic institutions, a play upon space bound by its own fixity. At the same time, unless these spaces bear distinct connections to the systemic core of democratic institutions, their

Figures 4 and 5: *Supersurfaces. Courtesy of Sophia Vyzoviti* © *2009.*

ability to effect institutional change is compromised. For example, bloggers are able to exert power to the extent that they success-fully capture the attention of mainstream media or a critical mass. YouTube videos are included in the agenda of public affairs only after, and provided, they go viral. Participants in online political discussion groups feel more gratified and engage when politicians are involved in the conversation, thus suggesting a connection for the group to the systemic conventions of democracy (e.g., Jankowski and van Selm, 2000). The concept communicates both the *empowerment* enabled via the production of multiple reflexive spaces and the challenges offered by spaces that are organically generated, and thus may not always support direct systemic con-nections to core societal institutions.

Folded, fragmented, reconnected, woven, and regenerated struc-tures present space that is multiplied and flexible. Fluid and multiplied spaces are remixed and further remixable, light and reflexive. This liquidity of space permits a variety of uses, but, in a democratic context, it also negates or redefines the ability of these spaces to afford power. Within convergent supersurfaces several realities and audiences either overlap, or share the self as the focal point of reference.

As a result, it is possible that a sense of space, physical and social, may be misplaced. For this reason, individuals may go to great lengths, determined by the affordances of technologies, to re-insert situational definition to their converged experiences. For example, virtual social environments, like Second Life or Twinity, are structured around a combination of "sociability and experi-mentation" (Castells, 2009, p. 69). On SNSs, online technologies are employed so as to finesse the details of self-expression online. On MySpace and Friendster, displays of interests are carefully selected and arranged so as to communicate affiliation with a par-ticular taste culture or fabric, thus conveying a sense of situational and cultural belonging (Liu, Maes, & Davenport, 2006; Liu, 2007). For members of a YouTube community, "publicly private" (private behaviors, exhibited with the member's true identity) and "pri-vately public" (sharing publicly accessible video without disclosing the member's true identity) behaviors are manipulated to signal different depths of relationships and to communicate empathy, respect, or inclusion among members of the network (Lange, 2007). For members of SNSs, belonging to some social networks over others communicates social status (Papacharissi, 2009). Furthermore, communication modes are employed to convey social identity and the authenticity of that identity on online social networks (Donath & boyd, 2004; Donath, 2007). Adept performances, however, require some mastery of the expressive equipment at hand, or the ability to maneuver in what Castells (2001) termed the *technical geography*. The ability to edit, or *redact*, one's own, multiple self-performances may re-associate the individual with a sense of place. As such, redactional acumen becomes a survival skill, as individuals balance performances across converged places. A sense of place helps navigate through convergent supersurfaces; however, this sense of place is individually arrived at and exercised, with the self as the central point of reference.

Across these multiplied and confluent planes of activity, identity may still be place-shaped, but is seldom place-based. Thus, the self develops along what de Certeau (1984) terms a *moving map*, which denotes both connection to space and the fluidity of this space. Places, however, gain symbolic meaning as they become the site of activity that is socially, culturally, politically, and economically infused. As places converge and multiply, what happens to activities that were previously exclusive to the static places of work, home, leisure, polity, and commerce and thus at least provisionally separated?

Convergence of practices

While it is important to understand the opportunities that convergent technologies afford us, it is also necessary to remind ourselves that several of the socio-cultural shifts associated with technology are variably experienced by populations, depending on historical and geographical context. For some populations, space, and by consequence activity housed within that space, has become converged and more fluid. Still, there remain activities that are place-based and exist because of their connection to a particular place. These may be activities of a political nature (voting), socio-cultural nature (marriage), economic nature (trading of non-information goods and services), or legal nature (trial and punishment, citizenship) that are all characterized by association with a particular space. However, as boundaries previously separating the spheres on which these activities occurred are collapsed or multiplied, several activities associated with the work sphere, the home, public life, commerce, and other social landscapes are consequently converged. And several place-based activities stretch over the mediated landscape afforded by mobile and confluent technology.

The results are complex and varied. Some are associated with evolving divisions between private and public places that lead to activities generally structured for the (privately public or publicly private) social. Concurrently, several of the symbols or habits we associate with that which is social, cultural, political, and economic are broadcast over a multiplicity of mediated environments, the nature of which is both homogeneous and fragmented. As Melucci (1999) suggests, the convergence of information flows "ties the world system together and . . . inflates the issues and arenas of conflict into worldwide proportions," thus rendering "the geographical localization of a problem [of] secondary importance," and reactivating "ethnic and local conflicts that seek to give a stable and recognizable basis to identity in a space that has lost its traditional boundaries" (p. 416). The abstract categories of social, cultural, political, economic, and other topical activities are operationalized through activities pursued, which are then ascribed that particular label. As the physical and virtual geographies along which these activities are formulated multiply and converge, the texture of what was once defined as social, cultural, political, and so forth is subsequently inflected. For some, this implies little distinction between sites of labor and leisure, or work and the domestic sphere (Andrejevic, 2004; Castells, 2001; Moores, 2004). In other cases, the social and the political are blurred, as mediated environments fail to distinguish between the two. Political candidates are covered by the news on the basis of their political record of achievement as well as their social character and repertoire of morally related decision-making (Jamieson, 2003; Patterson, 1993; Thompson,

2000). Successful blogs like The Huffington Post offer a menu of news items covering hard, soft, and pop news all in the same blurb. Blogs like The Daily Kos that offer more politically concentrated coverage do so from a personalized perspective. Popular sites like YouTube or Digg offer no topical categorization besides that determined by recency or popularity. Websites that are strictly social, political, cultural or economic are rare. Physical spaces that are specifically dedicated to commerce (shops), sociability (cafés), culture (museums), and politics (civic centers, government buildings) are variably remediated into arenas that combine a range of activities.

This does not imply a wholly new trend, nor does it imply that these spheres of activity were much more neatly divided in the past. On the contrary, past ideals of political engagement carried an expressed socio-cultural component and were frequently situated in markets or centers of economic activity. So the trend is not new. Nor is it indicative of a less fulfilling mode of existence. But the intensity of the trend is compounded by fluid technology that affords an architecture that makes it easier for these categories of societal organization to become even more fluid and elusive. Thus, the organizational foundation of our everyday ecologies, elusively defined to begin with, becomes more slippery.

The resulting environment of converged practices further augments a traditionally slippery relationship we have had with *the political*. Mouffe (in Miessen, 2007) argues that liberal thought has never been able to conform to the "specificity of the political. When liberals intend to speak about politics, they either think in terms of economics . . . or in terms of morality . . . but what is specific to the political always eludes liberal thought . . . to be able to act in politics one needs to understand what is the dynamic of the political" (http:// roundtable.kein.org/node/545, accessed April 2009). The political becomes even more elusive in the context of converged media and the converged expression these media afford. Concurrently, as the shift towards consensus politics minimizes ideological differences among parties, political factions become voter-oriented rather than member-oriented (Dahlgren, 2009), thus further removing ideology from that which we define as political.

The cultural logic behind this global trend of constant revolution and subsequent adjustment has been described as liquid modernity (Bauman, 2005) or reflexivity (Giddens, 1990). In this sense, social practices are re-examined and reformed on the basis of incoming information in a reflexive manner, thus rendering the necessity of fixed labels obsolete. These reflexive practices are pieced together to form narratives that may reference but are not specified by rigid categories, as these are liquid and evolving, and are interrupted as new social institutions and forms are revised. In this state of constant revolution, individuals are required to be flexible and adapt, and decisions are frequently arrived at via calculation of projected risk and future development, rather than through affiliation with solidified discourses of state, religion, and morality that are no longer static (Bauman, 2000, 2005; Beck, 1992; Giddens, 1990). In liquid modernity, *the political* becomes more elusive, as there exist no longer sites that are anchored to politics, confirming what Arendt termed an *emptiness of political space*.

In contrast to the fluidity of late modernity, however, social form retains the labels and narratives associated with preceding forms of societal organization. So, in the face of liquid uncertainty and reflexive shape-shifting, we still evoke frames of reference that have long since evolved. We lament that we no longer practice civic engagement, as it was practiced by our ancestors. We are surprised by our ever-developing cynicism, despite millennia of intelligent existence and experiences that afford us this very skepticism. We are concerned that our actions narcissistically revolve around the politics of self-interest, yet, at the same time, the self is the one constant in the midst of ongoing reflexivity. Finally, we exist in a social realm of mass-produced images and symbols made relevant to us primarily through a sphere of consumption, which we process in a manner that is both, in Benkler's terms (2006), *plastic and critical*. In this convergent sphere of experiences, space is colonized by activities that combine the social, commercial, political, and cultural, but do not define them in isolation.

At the same time, the search for activities that are purely of a political nature runs counter to human impulse and is maybe somewhat impractical. Humans rarely convene to discuss matters that are solely political, then neatly dispersing into social or other activities when political affairs are taken care of. Individuals discuss politics among and together with other things, and this practice helps them connect politics to essential parts of their everyday routines. Political life has developed out of the human need for sociability, and, as such, it adopts the practices and pace of social life.

Technology as the architecture of the new

It is also possible that our quest for civic behaviors has not produced the desired results because we have not been looking at places that civic behaviors now inhabit: spaces that are friendlier to the development of contemporary civic behaviors. Some advise that we advance beyond the political sphere to the social sphere (Lii, 1998; Sassi, 2000) and search the realm of sociality for the citizen's lost political soul. As the boundaries of public and private are reshaped and the form of family and work is reorganized, a new set of socio-political habits of cultural relevance and economic merit is developing. Beck (1997) describes this as a new political society that reinvents politics, as many issues covering technology, the environment, the family, gender relations, work, and globalizations now belong to the realm of politics, and are served through a variety of activities and spheres. This new politics is specific to our times and develops in cognition of, but beyond, labels of East and West, left and right, political and social, economic and cultural. The traditional aggregate/representative and deliberative models of democracy can no longer sufficiently explain newer political developments and movements, ranging from a revival of fundamentalism to environmental policymaking.

Thus, *the political* may be located in a sphere that is more about conflict and the deliberation of a plurality of issues and perspectives, and less about typical labels that categorize and organize political action (Mouffe, 2005). This prioritizes an exchange of opinion and disconnects *the political* from the search for consensus. An agonistic pluralism lies at the heart of the political, and "can contribute to subverting the ever-present temptation existing in democratic societies to naturalize its frontiers and essentialize its identities" (Mouffe, 2005, p. 105). In the context of contemporary democracies, there is no institutionalized political arena where the political resides. Instead, it is reflexively articulated through discursive practices, which allow the formulation of both agonistically framed arguments, and agonistically exercised claims to power. It is in this contemporary architecture, more reflective of current relations between power, ideology, and identity that convergent technologies contribute to liquid and ever-evolving, ever-imperfect democracies and citizens.

4

The Question of Citizenship in a Converged Environment

> The nature of citizenship, like that of the state, is a question which is often disputed: there is no general agreement on a single definition.
>
> Aristotle, in *Politics* [384–322 BC] (2004)

The problem of defining citizenship is not new. The concept of citizenship possesses a long history and a complicated legacy. Never divorced from context, citizenship presents an abstract ideal put in place to describe how individuals could contribute to the affairs of the polity. Citizenship has thus presupposed engagement with civic affairs and is prescriptive of modes that individuals follow to connect to the sphere of politics and public administration. Modalities of practicing citizenship evolve as economic, socio-cultural, and political schematics further mature. The private-property-bound and race/gender/class-restricted models of citizenship prevalent in the Ancient Greco-Roman eras stipulated explicit and prescribed civic obligations. By contrast, models of citizenship that developed in the Middle Ages associated religious piety with civic duty. Republican models of citizenship re-asserted civic rights, and modern models of citizenship frequently locate civic activity in the consumer sphere. The singularity of citizenship to a unique era redefines past perceptions of civic involvement and sets the tone for models of civic involvement to follow.

The sensitivity of the concept of citizenship to historical and cultural context requires an examination of conditions that precede it. Citizenship contours the map with which individuals navigate democracy. It specifies civic behaviors across public and private boundaries. It utilizes technology as a means of equipping citizens with the tools with which to deliberate on, make, and act upon informed decisions. Citizenship is reified upon public and private territory, and is defined by our evolving understandings of public and private divisions. In addition, the mythos of new technology infuses civic hopes, thoughts, and action with narratives of what good citizenship should be like. Convergent technologies, with their inherent ability to multiply and pluralize expression, afford endless possibilities for citizens, but do they complicate or render effortless the practice of citizenship?

This chapter poses the question of what (good) citizenship means in a converged media environment. The concept of citizenship is examined and defined, and previous models of citizenship are reviewed and related to developments in contemporary democracies (Kivisto & Faist, 2007). The complex connection of citizenship to capitalist modes of production and late modernity is explicated (Dean, 2003; Inglehart & Welzel, 2005; van Steenbergen, 1994), as it informs contemporary incarnations of civil society, the rhetoric of globalization and cosmopolitanism, the overlap of consumer culture and civic practices (Habermas, 2004; Miller, 2007), and expectations of civic engagement and social capital generated (Putnam, 2001; Schudson, 1998). It is with an understanding of the historical progression of citizenship, as well as with insight into the conditions of modernity and capitalism, that the role of the citizen in a converged digital environment is sketched out. Previous models of civic engagement are used to understand whether and how this breed of citizen is unique.

A long history of imperfect citizenship

Citizenship presents an evolving and contextual process. It captures the state of mind from which individuals report to civic duties at hand. As civic duties transform and democracies mature, the texture of citizenship shifts shape, but its connection to democracy remains constant. Its centrality to democracy is not disputed, nor is it possible for citizenship to vanish. But it is possible for the activities that define citizenship to reform and relocate away from modes of civic engagement that have come to be considered traditional. This does not imply the end of citizenship; it simply points to new modes of civic engagement that are emerging. It has become habitual in contemporary democracies to lament that there are no citizens. Michael Schudson (1998) actually traced the first instance of this complaint to the eighteenth century and the work of Jean-Jacques Rousseau, who observed that "We have physicists, geometers, chemists, astronomers, poets, musicians, and painters; we no longer have citizens" (Rousseau, 1750, as cited in Schudson, 1998, p. 365). Schudson recorded this as the first proclamation of the end of citizenship, but this also presents a first attempt at associating the ascent of the professional sphere and the workplace with a possible displacement of civic activity that previously resided in spheres now occupied by professions.

This concern then re-emerges in a variety of writings by intellectuals and academics affiliated with political science, sociology, and communication. De Tocqueville (1835/1840), despite his admiration for the American model of democratic equality, expressed concerns about the incompatibility of a material culture that prioritized seeking material security with the independent pursuit of intellectual freedom. Dewey (1927) was hopeful about the role of communication and journalism in energizing a Great Public, but also concerned about the influence of commercial hegemony. Lippmann (1925) worried that individual members of the public were much too self-centered to care about public policy, and were frequently summoned to contribute to democracy through formulaic exercises, which merely required that they "do as little as possible in matters where they can do nothing very well" (p. 198). C. Wright Mills (1953, 1956) cautioned that mass society communication channels prescribe civic engagement that is so organized as to often effectively render individuals disinterested observers or "strangers to politics" (p. 328). Riesman (1950) located these behaviors in his citizen type of the *indifferent*: spectator citizens whose politics is driven by a consumerist approach and whose beliefs frequently reside in the "Don't Know" polling response. Sennett (1970) connected civic passivity to the excessively organized order of modern urban living and the subsequent rise of a new Puritanism. Lasch (1979) explained civic apathy as a symptom of materially driven self-absorption and evolving narcissism.

Putnam (1996) traced the historical progression of citizenship in the modern era to structure a similar argument, finding television guilty of displacing time previously devoted to community involvement more generative of social capital. This sequence of citizenship critiques progresses in reverse-direction reproducible irony: Putnam (1996) idealizes the great civic generations that Riesman and Mills had dubbed indifferent; Riesman and Mills confront civic indifference as a condition singular to the socio-economic hierarchy of their era, implying a comparison with a past ideal state. Yet, in that past state, Lippmann and Dewey had already expressed concern over the indifference of citizens, and had delved into the past in search of an ideal community, a past which de Tocqueville, and, before him, Rousseau, had also surveyed to no avail, in pursuit of the missing citizen.

The quest for the good citizen is ongoing. Private property and its conflicting relationship to intellectual freedom, the socio-economic order of capitalism, the hegemonic and formulaic structure of engaging the public in later modernity, the commercial structure of mass media, and the conditions of living in late modernity, all present explanations for why the citizen has gone missing. The explanations overlap, complement, or contradict each other, but they all have one thing in common: the belief that, at a certain point in our past, a form of perfect citizenship existed. Nostalgia for this past ideal of citizenship is sequentially reproduced in the writings of intellectuals who fail to locate perfect citizenship in their contemporary eras, and reference in reverse chronological order practices of citizenship that had already been condemned by their intellectual predecessors as inadequate.

Dating back to Ancient Greece, Aristotle defined citizenship as the essence of human being, but lived in a society that did not grant the privilege of citizenship to everyone. The question then revolves around whether citizenship presents an ideal residing mostly in the academic, intellectual, and, by extension, collective imagination. Are we mourning the collapse of a civic state that never existed, and are we then subsequently doomed to citizenship that is destined to be forever imperfect?

A historical overview of the transitions that models of citizenship have gone through should help at least to contextualize these concerns. Citizenship is a representation of socio-political identity, which pertains specifically to how individuals relate to the administration of public affairs. For most humans, citizenship is one of many roles we take on as we associate with others and society. The identity that has been a principal influence in how individuals interpret their own citizenship is nationhood. In addition, different systems of governance – including the feudal system, oligarchy, monarchy, and tyranny – devise different forms of connecting to their citizens. It is in a democratic system, however, that the potential of the citizen, in terms of how s/he is involved in the administration of public affairs, is optimized. In democratic systems, the conditions of autonomy, equality, and participation in the affairs of the polity define the role of the democratic citizen, and present the focus of this indicative, but not exhaustive, overview.

Scholars adopt a variety of approaches when undertaking a synthesis of models of citizenship, but most models are rooted in Aristotle's understanding of a human and a citizen as a *political animal*. For the Ancient Greeks, being a citizen was a natural state of being. For the Romans, citizenship expressed man's legal ties to the state, and that is where the roots of a citizen as subject of the state can be located (Pocock, 1995). Another possible distinction between forms of socio-political identity reflected by distinct models of citizenship is presented by Marshall (Marshall & Bottomore, 1992), who argued for the following three forms of citizenship, presented in historical order: civil, political, and social. Civil citizenship specifies the equality of all subjects before the law, political citizenship builds on legal citizenship and provides citizens with the privilege of a vote, and social citizenship prescribes the welfare state. Several have found this tripartite distinction to be founded upon a Westernized perspective on civic engagement; however, it is meaningful as a categorization of civic rights (Heater, 2004; Kivisto & Faist, 2007). Remaining models of citizenship are broad and general, either focusing on first-wave citizenship, based around small-scale societies, and second-wave citizenship, constructed around eighteenth-century revolutions, or distinguishing between civic Republican and alternative liberal models of civic involvement (Heater, 2004; Schwarzmantel, 2003). The latter is reflective of the greater civic Republican and liberal traditions, and resurfaces in most works examining the contemporary relevance of citizenship.

The civic Republican model relies upon citizen civic virtue and a virtuous state republic. Both citizens and the republic of the state must act justly and with the greater goal of being good, or virtue (*areté*), in mind. A community of good citizens cannot be envisioned without the presence of a magnanimous and fair state that is a republic, and a republic cannot truly function without committed citizens motivated by civic virtue, thus resulting in a *civic Republican* citizen (Heater, 2004; Schwarzmantel, 2003). The civic Republican model dominates the first wave of citizenship, whereas the alternative liberal model evolves with the social turmoil and revolution of the seventeenth and eighteenth centuries, and becomes solidified during the industrial and post-industrial eras. The liberal model specifies that the state must ensure that all citizens possess and enjoy civic, political, and social rights freely. Both models designate specific duties for the citizen and state, and are suggestive of a different balance of economic, political, social, and cultural affairs. Whereas the civic republican model positions civic virtue as the end goal of the polity and vaguely associates it with the common good, the liberal model specifically defines this common good as the assurance that all citizens freely enjoy civic, political, and social rights, provided and protected by the state, and assumes that civic duties will emerge out of the possession of those rights. Thus, we have the roots of two enlightened but broad understandings of citizenship, which are timeless enough to adjust to historical and cultural context, but are also amorphous enough to be subject to the interpretations of evolving intellectual thought.

The first traces of the idea of citizenship lead back to the city-state of Sparta, known for its ascetic model of citizenship, employed within an oligarchic and totalitarian model that relied on slavery for economic labor, as well as on the equal participation of privileged elites to manage affairs of the state with the greater goal of civic virtue in mind. In Sparta we find the origins of economic, social, and constitutional reform directed at effecting collective governance, even if that was to be administered by a select few in a society that prioritized military imperatives.

Plato, inspired by the reforms of the Spartan system, proposed the idea of the *polis*, or the city-state, relieved citizens of economic labor, and advanced the idea of a representative elite or council, appointed by the citizen classes. He was drawn to the idea of civic virtue, but distanced his reflections from the militaristic culture of Sparta. Where Plato was consumed with drafting an ideal polity, Aristotle's approach was more pragmatic, and concerned with understanding the actual and everyday principles driving citizenship. He toiled with the concepts of "ruling" and civic virtue, seeking to sketch the parameters that would enable individuals to co-exist during the hard times of war, but mostly in leisure and peace. Aristotle's ideal of democracy combined popular rule with the advice of wise and experienced experts, thus carving a role for elites in democratic governance. But he understood citizenship as a deeply human condition, a natural state of mind for most humans. This natural state of being did not involve work; it was the absence of economic labor and the delegation of that to slaves that enabled men to devote themselves to the pursuits of citizenship and an active life in the polity. Those possessing the privilege of citizenship in Ancient Greece and Rome did not have to work.

The Romans were equally drawn to the idea of civic virtue (*virtus*), but mainly interested in solidifying the legal base of citizenship. It was the Stoics and Cicero who, concerned with the decaying civic involvement of the upper classes, outlined civic duties and famously declared that life lived in private is a betrayal of social life and democracy, thus placing the citizen firmly in the public realm. The Stoics are further responsible for developing the idea of cosmopolitan or universal citizenship, originating from the Greek *kosmopolites*, which means "citizen of the world." In this sense, citizens are bound to the commonwealth of their city-state first, but also fulfill civic obligations connected to the greater commonwealth of the known world. These ideas define the understanding of citizenship as it is sustained during the Roman Empire. Still, critical thought on the nature of citizenship emerges out of discontent with the performance of civic duty and the desire to solidify democratic tradition in the midst of transition to newer forms of social organization.

During the Greco-Roman period, citizenship presented a focal point of democratic government and the primary means for individuals to serve the *polis*. The growing spread of Christianity ascribed a religious component to civic duty, which cast individuals as servants to God first, thus primarily associating virtue or *areté* with religious piety, and less so with the public good. During the Middle Ages, as the Church led the State in the administration of public affairs, citizenship attained merely peripheral importance, except in the Italian city-states of Florence, Venice, Bologna, and others that maintained senates, councils, voting rights, and variable assortments of republican features of governance. It was during this time of feudal states and absolute monarchy models that citizenship became firmly connected to nationhood, and citizens were viewed primarily as a ruler's subjects. Heater (2004) notes that, in the sixteenth century, citizenship was revisited as a way of enhancing sovereignty and the stability of the strong nation-states of Britain, France, and Spain that were emerging. Monarchs granted restricted rights to citizens as a way of reconciling subjects and citizens, connecting both more firmly to the priorities of the nation-state. Much literature on the concept of *civility* emerges at this stage, as civil behavior describes the connection of citizens to the nation-state, but has little to do with enjoying the merits of citizenship at the time. Yet again, as throughout the course of history, the concept of citizenship bends to adjust to and reflect changes in the balance of socio-political power.

The seventeenth and eighteenth centuries bear witness to intellectual activity that seeks to revive the classical republican model of citizenship, and connects it to the responsibilities of the state, thus laying the groundwork for the socio-political revolutions that followed and the liberal model of citizenship that emerged out of them. Locke's work formulated the basis for several of these developments by firmly placing civil rights on the political agenda, and defining such rights as inclusive of the right to live, the right to be free, and the right to private property. Rousseau's ideas laid the foundation for the principles of civic association, culminating with the *Social Contract*, in which he located the right to equal liberty, the pursuit of the General Will, and fraternity at the center of a social contract binding all citizens in equality and liberty for all. His work planted the seeds of the liberal model of citizenship, but it was not until the American Revolution, the result of the combination of Puritan asceticism and dedication to equal rights and access to wealth for all, that European-spawned revolutions united citizens in pursuit of these rights, in addition to the rights to vote and to hold office.

Consequently, these rights were pursued by all groups previously excluded from public governance, including women and racial minorities. Socio-cultural revolutions of the twentieth century connect civil rights to citizenship status, and experiment with different economic models that may guarantee equal rights, but also equal freedom, social power, and wealth, for all. The advent of industrialism, capitalism, the urbanization of the economy, and the subsequent socio-cultural adjustment from a collective (*Gesellschaft*) to an individualized (*Gemeinschaft*) state of being led to further alignments in the way we understand and practice our civic duty in the contemporary eras. Modernity and late modernity produce models of citizenship that reflect the intersection of capitalist, consumerist, and liberal narratives, as they combine to suggest an unexpected mix of civic modalities that typify citizenship, and are examined in the following section. Yet, this condensed overview underlines the fluidity of citizenship, which evolves gradually and reciprocally with societal modes of organization and change.

The past and contemporary citizenship modalities

It becomes apparent that citizenship is never perfectly practiced. In Ancient Greco-Roman times, civilians were excused from economic labor in order to perform their duties as citizens, hence the paradox of a democracy constructed around slave labor. In the Middle Ages, the Church, feudalism, and states rely on the work of loyal subjects for the generation of economic capital, and the meaning and practice of citizenship become convoluted into religiously fueled nationalist and imperialist rhetoric. Public intellectuals and socio-political revolutions of the seventeenth, eighteenth, and nineteenth centuries sought to restore and guarantee citizen rights for working civilians. But the relationship between the generation of capital, the distribution of power, and the dominant ideology of an era come to define the models of citizenship that emerge and the civic duties that are pursued (Schwarzmantel, 2003). Perfect or good citizenship remains elusive, although the ideal of striving towards civic virtue remains a collective vision. Emerging practices of citizenship surface as reactions to power struggles, economic imbalances, and social inequalities, with the long-term goal of equitable public governance. Citizenship flexes and adjusts, to correspond to the historical context that it inhabits.

To this point, Kivisto and Faist (2007) find it more meaningful to understand citizenship as a general concept employed to communicate patterns of exclusion, inclusion, erosion of past practices, withdrawal from civic engagement, and adjustment of citizenship to historically sensitive conditions. In this sense, citizenship is a process that advances through history as a reflection of civic trends and the connections these civic trends bear to democracy. Still, because our struggle, as a human species, to understand and secure equal civic rights for all has been so gradual, long, and imperfect, we are puzzled by contemporary displays of civic apathy, or alienation from the world of politics. It is mystifying that we would publicly express disinterest in the same civic privileges that preoccupied our ancestors for so long.

Yet it is not disinterest in citizenship that we express. Nor does apathy reflect disregard for the rights to freedom and free will, the vote, private property, public governance, and the pursuit of happiness and virtue. Apathy expresses distaste for the conditions within which we are summoned to practice civic duty. Disinterest describes fatigue with habits that are several hundreds of years old. Finally, we are burdened with social and economic responsibilities that our ancestors, responsible for the civic legacy that holds us hostage with civic duty prescriptions from other eras, did not contend with. Buckingham (2000), in trying to understand political alienation among the young, argued that, rather than bemoaning ignorance of public affairs, we should rethink what counts as civic engagement in political societies and redefine citizenship to include newer modes of civic engagement that are emerging. In the next few pages, I review contemporary modalities of citizenship, and examine how reflective they may be of a model of citizenship that is imperfect, but, of our own and contemporary times.

The citizen consumer

Civic engagement in modern and late modern democracies is characterized by a somewhat opaque understanding of what qualifies as civic, frequently dimmed further by the conceptual proximity of the civic to the social, the political, the cultural, and neighboring spheres of activity. The ascent of consumption as a form of identity expression only complicates civic duty further, as acts of consumption frequently enable modern citizens to express political identity. The prevalence of a consumer culture is the cornerstone of many explanations provided by sociologists, political scientists, and communication scholars who connect contemporary civic disinterest to a culture that prioritizes the pursuit of materialistic goals. Of interest here are the precise activities that delineate the citizen consumer as a distinct type of citizen, and the civic merit associated with these activities.

Lizbeth Cohen (2003) traced the origins of civically located consumerist behaviors in *A Consumer's Republic*, creating a historical context for the gradual commercialization of civic behaviors. The origins of the citizen consumer are located in the era of the Great Depression, in the context of which consumption was encouraged as a means of boosting the economy and perceived as patriotic. In the same vein, during the Second World War, the act of consumption was cultivated as an act of sustaining the economy and doing battle on the home front. In the 1950s, a mass-consumption utopia was presented to the American public as an alternative route to a democracy of equal access to all goods and services, attainable through the combined forces of commerce, media, advertising, and marketing. Thus the act of consumption is connected to prosperity, creating new jobs, and supporting the American way of life in a manner that renders consumption in post-war America "not [a] personal indulgence, but rather a civic responsibility" (Cohen, 2003, p. 113). Consumption becomes equated with serving the public good. The private marketplace emerges as the primary terrain of this civil society. At the same time, the firm connection established between consumption and citizenship presented several marginalized groups, and especially African Americans, with a commercially grounded avenue for fighting discrimination and claiming their place as citizens in this republic. Thus, the economic ability to consume is redrafted as civic responsibility, and framed as a route to civic privileges, otherwise not accessible to those not able to consume or without a home (Hebdige, 1993).

Although home ownership and mass consumption signaled a move to a more egalitarian society, the imperatives of the marketplace frequently spun these settings into a self-sustaining economic narrative that tended to undercut social commitment to the wellbeing of the masses. Gradually, the growth and model of suburban expansion and home ownership created civic community spheres, but also recreated inequalities associated with the economic distribution of privilege in the suburbs. Suburban cultures appropriated civic behaviors to sustain the vibrancy, and thus economic viability, of the suburb. Suburbanization was further facilitated through a mass privatization, that is, commercialization, of public spaces like shopping malls and meeting places, wherein community and consumption gradually came to be perceived as conflicting ends. This trend is reversed with the suburbanization of cities, the further segmentation of suburban and urban markets, and the proliferation of niche audiences. Objectives of community and consumption are therefore further blurred in both urban and suburban areas. The culmination of consumption as a civic act is effected as the endorsement or rejection of commercial goods and services becomes associated with the expression of political will.

Several critiques attribute the demise of civic life and rise of civic narcissism to the intertwining of citizen and consumer roles definitive of American public life (Lasch, 1979). The production and consumption of mediated content further compounds the effect of consumer culture on civic life, as the line between audiences and publics is blurred (Ettema & Whitney, 1994; Hay, Grossberg, & Wartella, 1996). Audiences are reified on the basis of their consumption habits, while consuming publics are generated by employing reference frames that are increasingly mediated. Increasingly, individuals are "hailed" or interpellated primarily as potential consumers and less often as citizens (Althusser, 1970/1998), in cultures both private and public, across planes that are dedicated to consumption, or public life, or both (Ang, 1996; McCarthy, 2001), within a consumption-dominated habitus that shapes and is shaped by identity-affirming practices, including of course civic ones (Bourdieu, 1977). Convergent channels of communication are remediated into a sphere of consumption constructed by traditional and mainstream media. Thus, forms of civic expression that develop on converged platforms, including YouTube, blogs, and video blogs (vlogs), become civic exercises in "consumer-style critique," symptomatic of a hedonistic and materialistic culture (Scammell, 2000, p. 354).

Still, if consumption has become so ingrained into our everyday routines and intertwined with civic practices, it may be unrealistic to expect a decoupling of consumer and citizen roles. While a hardcore Habermasian would reject the possibility of compatibility between consumer and citizen roles, one questions whether separating the two would inherently guarantee a renewed sense of civic duty. But the question I pose is: if consumption is such a fundamental characteristic of modern and late modern democracies, then what would a contemporary citizen do to practice civic duty in the absence of a consumer culture? In response, Canclini (2001) finds that intertwined consumer and citizen states are informed by a complex set of transterritorial and multilingual cultures that vie for the attention of the consuming citizen and shape post-modern identities: "Instead of basing themselves on oral and written communications that circulated in personalized spaces characterized by close interaction, these identities take shape in relation to the industrial production of culture, its communications technologies, and the differentiated and segmented consumption of commodities" (p. 29). The citizen consumer should be able to reorganize and recompose the fragmented sequence of commodities into a coherent narrative that expresses citizenship in the contemporary era. From this perspective, Castells (1977) places contemporary consumption far from mass-motivated compulsion and close to an *interactive socio-political rationality*, the site of contemporary class conflict. Therefore, if the site of late modern class struggle is the locus of consumption, how is it natural for the citizen to be much removed from it? Canclini (2001) suggests that consumption is good for thinking, as "to consume is to participate in an arena of competing claims for what society produces and the ways of using it . . . a space of interaction where producers and senders no longer simply seduce their audiences; they also have to justify themselves rationally" (p. 39).

I do not suggest that consumption in late modern democracies presents the equivalent of citizenship. Nor do I imply that all civic activities are rooted in the sphere of consumption. I do wish to highlight, however, the tendency to define terms associated with civic practice, including the meaning of the public, the citizen, and civic merit, using language reflective of eighteenth-century civic habits and irrelevant to the everyday realities of contemporary citizens. If indeed consumption presents such a corrosive force to civic virtue, then what better way to confront it and reshape it as citizens of a democracy than by redefining civic duty and practice to include and confront the sphere of the commercial? Citizenship in past democracies may not have been colonized by the consumerist rhetoric of mass post-industrialized societies, but it, too, had its own demons, which civic duty adjusted to in order to confront (Schudson, 1998). Dean (2003) suggests that contemporary citizenship be reified via a mode corrective of the "hubris emerging from the revitalized marriage of capitalism and science," thus providing a way out of civic cul-de-sacs into which the consumption-oriented citizen is driven (p. 181). While technology may cultivate the civic imagination and capitalism will continue as the dominant means of organizing the economies of societies, civic ethics may become the domain of the citizen whose civic duties include rectifying the ideological monopoly of consumption. These new civic obligations may be met via a variety of practices which evolve beyond the public/private binary to that of the social, thus suggesting a civic sociality that guides citizens enabled within a consumer's republic.

Ideals of civic engagement that we frequently evoke were developed in the context of *poleis* radically different from the ones we inhabit nowadays. Yet, while we ably describe our contemporary crossroads of capitalist, consumerist, transnational, localized, mediated, and political narratives, we neglect to update narrative vocabularies of citizenship. Silverstone (2007) proposed the *mediapolis* as the site where the contemporary citizen self-actualizes. The mediapolis is not dependent on a specific location, and consists of the mediated public space, commercial and not, where contemporary civic activity develops. The mediapolis is less than the public sphere but more than mere public space, as it is grounded and shaped by the sphere of the media, and thus bears "no integrity," as "it is fractured by cultural difference and the absence of communication, as much as it is by the homogenization of global television and genuine, if only momentary, collective attention to global events, crises and catastrophes" (p. 31). Through this space of socio-technical appearance, the media present a version of a world, that, in the absence of direct experience, effectively constitutes *the* world. Media power is central to the articulation of this space, but it does not render this space apolitical, as the mediapolis remains a space, imperfect yet necessary, where political positions are expressed and negotiated by parties of varying power, and where narratives of consumption are dominant. Rather than continuing to struggle with a distinction between consumption and citizenship, contemporary citizenship narratives should root the citizen firmly in the mediapolis, and, if they must prescribe, then assign civic duty that bears relevance to the contemporary realities of power struggle and conflict.

Cultural citizenship

In the multicultural and transnational context of globalized societies, the concept of cultural citizenship emphasizes the centrality of culture to globally exercised civic duties. Cultural citizenship is connected to a cosmopolitan awareness of and respect for all cultures, but is also inclusive of intercultural and intra-cultural reference frames that make up a contemporary citizen profile. More than anything, cultural citizenship implies that the primary means of expression for citizens are delivered through culture and cultural reference, ranging from popular culture to cross-cultural, intra-cultural, and transnational points of reference. Concurrently, because in late modern democracies culture is mediated by commercial and mass institutions, these forms of civically motivated cultural expression frequently reside in the terrain of consumption of goods and services, and are accessed via viewership of mediated cultural content. For citizen consumers, consumption is a civic exercise. Cultural citizenship differs from the citizen as consumer mode, as it pertains specifically to the employment of culture, popular, national, or consumer, for claims to citizenship and for the expression and fulfillment of civic needs.

Cultural citizenship is claimed in response to a crisis of belonging, attributed to a decline in traditional forms of civic engagement, the erosion of the news sphere, and the permeation of consumption into all aspects of everyday life. Miller (2007) postulates seven formations, articulated in previous research and historical examinations, that theorize the phenomenon of cultural citizenship in the context of complex politics that has given rise to it. First, he emphasizes the need for liberal governments to acknowledge social-movement identities, as a way of recognizing the economic opportunities afforded by globalization, but at the same time to formally preserve local heritage and the right to participate in it. Second, he connects cultural citizenship to collectively shared and individual human rights which define it as "a development from, and antidote to, assimilationist ideals" (Miller, 2007, p. 67). Third, he perceives this form of citizenship as a way to preserve the sovereignty of minority cultures. Fourth, education and awareness, along with formal recognition, of cultural citizenship status become the dominant means of granting and enabling cultural citizenship. Fifth, government-led efforts assume the task of monitoring the condition of cultural citizenship to ensure that conflicting ideologies do not compromise access to it. The sixth formation recognizes the limits of democracy, neoliberalism, and the free market economy, and the possibility that the limits of these can be addressed and amended or augmented by cultural difference, the result of which could be revolutionary. Finally, a seventh formation around the concept of cultural citizenship forecasts that future conflicts will be neither political, nor economic, but primarily cultural. Miller (2007) refers to a multitude of reports, research data, expert opinion, institutional evidence, and current events to explain how these seven tendencies have come to be.

These seven formations, however, define the right to cultural citizenship politically, and acknowledge its connection to socio-economic conflict, but neglect to address the political economy of cultural citizenship directly. To this end, Miller (2007) suggests that cultural citizens be understood as political actors *and* complex consumers who frequently exert politicized interpretations or acts of consumption to claim cultural citizenship. Conversely, the same cultural citizens may find their home cultural territory colonized by commercial narratives of consumption that compromise, marginalize, or commercialize a given cultural identity. This is precisely where the media enter the equation, providing the territory where cultural citizenship contestations take place. Popular culture, reproduced through mediated content, frequently legitimizes the cultural heritage and lifestyle of previously marginalized societal groupings, thus granting these groupings equal citizen status on the basis of cultural membership. Yet, at the same time, either by incorporating these differences as merely cultural or otherwise mainstreaming them, it simultaneously contests the very same status it granted. Take, for example, the recently popularized Bravo network, known for several shows structured around the idea of the gay male as cultural expert, including popular shows like *Queer Eye for the Straight Guy*, or *Tim Gunn's Guide to Style*. Both shows present a cultural terrain in which the traditional power structure is reversed and the heterosexual male or female functions as the minority or the non-expert. Cultural lifestyle choices associated with homosexuality are portrayed as homonormative, that is as the dominant or normative way of being. Yet, at the same time, the potentially empowering contexts are frequently compromised with injections of cultural normativity designed to render the shows audience-friendly to a wider consumer market. Finally, by incorporating and presenting gay identity strictly on the basis of cultural merit, mediated content frequently prioritizes gay identity as a lifestyle choice with an explicit upwardly mobile and financially successful component, thus "muting" out the socio-political aspect of gay identity and gay rights (Papacharissi & Fernback, 2008; Sender, 2001).

Similar mediated and negotiated presentations of cultural identity successfully endorse the right to cultural citizenship and potentially nullify its legitimacy by presenting this right as a lifestyle choice, practiced through daily acts of consumption. The result is a seamless narrative that is appealing to a multitude of cultural citizens, and effectively interweaves patterns of consumption that seek to reinforce and reproduce the cultural terrain claimed by these citizens. As a result, cultural citizenship may become "naturalized," meaning that aspects of it that are comforting to the mainstream are emphasized over more troubling aspects of it, which are undercut or further marginalized. Cultural citizenship, as heralded by the media and the sphere of consumption, is frequently sanctioned on a commercial and aesthetic basis, while the discursive and politicized aspect of it is overridden by commercial priorities. Thus, the civic duty of the contemporary citizen lies in challenging the ethics of these commercially driven discourses.

Cosmopolite

In a globalized environment, citizens are tasked with civic duties of monitoring and possibly opining on civic affairs of a global nature. Rooted in local cultures, but subjected at the same time to global market, political, and socio-cultural imperatives, global citizens must not only master knowledge of global and local affairs, but should also be able to balance and negotiate global and local priorities, and obligations. Individual citizens frequently reconcile conflicting discourses of the global and local into hybrid cultures of the global, which allow them to reorganize fragments of global and local cultures that must coalesce into a semi-coherent narrative that serves as the basis of the self. It is through the creation and expression of hybrid cultures that contemporary global citizens flex their civic muscle, and democratic institutions develop and reform in late modernity (Canclini, 1995). The experiences that inform the decisions of contemporary citizens possess a connection to place, but also develop through the translocal identities of individuals, at once rooting identity in ethnic origin and connecting it to multi-nationality in ways not previously accessible to the majority of citizens (Appadurai, 1996).

As citizenship departs from the geographic locus of national identity, it becomes sensitized to civic cultures, routines, and expectations of multiple origins. The effects of globalization on civic duty are experienced by citizens who live a translocal life sharing physical connections to a multiplicity of locations, as well as by more geographically fixed citizens who must familiarize themselves with cultures that contemporary media environments bring them in direct contact with. Convergent technologies provide the networked capability that promotes a sense of connection among geographically remote places and the possibility of a networked public sphere (Benkler, 2006). For citizens, this presents a simulation of a globally networked *polis*, mediated through technology that invites them to observe as well as participate. For potential citizens of the (networked) world, the leap between observation and participation, though technologically afforded, is only enabled by a sense of multicultural fluency and cultural logic, frequently referred to as *cosmopolitanism*.

Rooted in the Cynics' and Stoics' philosophical movements in Ancient Greece, *cosmopolites* were defined as citizens of the world, possessing the ability to connect to outer circles through focus on concentric experiences shared in common with others. The idea resurfaces with a focus on hospitality in the works of Kant, Levinas, and Derrida, as a way of understanding ethical obligations to respond to different cultures and the generalized Other. Ulrich Beck (1997) defines the operating logic of globalization in direct opposition to nation-state politics as the mentality of late modern globalized economies and democracies. A cosmopolitanism vision involves acknowledging otherness on a variety of interactional planes, including: the otherness of those culturally different, the otherness of the future (and connection to a World Risk Society), the otherness of nature, the otherness of the object, and the otherness of other rationalities (Beck, 2006). Cosmopolitanism presents the foundation of global civil society, mapped out as the realm of the contemporary global citizen. Cosmopolitanism shares some common moral ground with universalism, but accepts that global relationships are formed around processes of both agreement and conflict. Unlike universalism, cosmopolitanism emanates from the institutionalized individuality that presents the *modus operandi* for citizens who construct life worlds by means of accumulated choices, formed in response to globally reflexive environments.

In individualized societies of global consequence, citizens are situated in networked environments that impose a sense of fragmented solidarity, rendering, in Bauman's (2001) words, individuals *united in difference*. Bauman (2001) explains that the lack of obvious sites offering a totality of political experience places individuals in political spaces that are "partial, segmented, task-oriented, time-limited interventions" (p. 93). In the context of fragmented and individualized political experiences, it is easy for polarization, tribalization and ethnic marginalization of political identities to develop, unless a cosmopolitan code of ethics ensures that "separate identities stop short of exclusivity, of a refusal to cohabit with other identities. This in turn requires abandoning the tendency to suppress other identities in the name of the self-assertion of one's own, while accepting, on the contrary, that it is precisely the guarding of other identities that maintains the diversity in which one's own uniqueness can thrive" (p. 94). This is the ethical foundation of globalization as expressed through a cosmopolitan vision. Cosmopolitan ethics then lend credence to a political agenda that forms in recognition of, but extraneously to, the priorities of the nation-states. This form of "meta-politics" or "politics of politics" (Beck, 2006) requires the basis of the political, the unity of politics, and states to be divorced from each other and reassembled through the individualized narratives of cosmopolitan actors and citizens.

Cosmopolitanism advocates, but does not guarantee, global

piety. It enhances plurality, contains the possibility of forced cosmopolitanism or *cosmopolitanization*, the possible institution of internationalism as a new form of nationalism, and utilizes a diplomacy of military humanism constructed around the threat of war (Beck, 2006). Moreover, it encapsulates inherent post-modern ironies concerned with the simultaneous rejection of nationalism and the definition of otherness by means of national identity and affiliation. It does not resolve inequalities of class and power, or, as Castells (2009) suggests, propose a solution, without identifying the processes through which a cosmopolitan culture may come to be. Ong (1999) has explained how Asian cultures and economies have blended strategies of migration and capital accumulation in ways that reflect the fluidity of globally traded capital and the subsequent tensions developed between global, national, and personal identities. Moreover, van Steenbergen (1994) describes the tension between post-modernity and modern citizenship as resolvable via a "cultural aesthetic [that] might simply involve the recognition and acceptance of extreme cultural fragmentation, the importance of local knowledge and cultures, the promotion of feminist recognition of the significance of emotional commitments to different cultural preferences, and the attempt to recognize rather than to incorporate various ethnic, regional, and subnational cultures" (p. 166). So, cosmopolitanism does not present the answer for citizens, engaged or apathetic, nor does it present an ideology with which to civically organize and navigate new globalized political obligations. The potential of a global civil society will forever be challenged by cosmopolitan aspirations and capitalist pragmatism (Falk, 1994). But the cosmopolitan imaginary does organize the political space upon which contemporary citizens exercise civic duty, and, as such, it maps a potentially fragmented, but radically different territory from those traversed by our civic predecessors. This civic territory is routinely surveyed by the citizen types described next.

The monitorial citizen

Discourses on the meaning of citizenship are frequently premised on the ideal of committed and goal-oriented civic activity. It is possible, however, to conceive of contemporary civic engagement as reactive, rather than consistently active. Permanent, uninterrupted, and inherently purposive civic activity runs counter to human nature, priorities, and the pace of informationalized society. Schudson (1998) reviewed the historical progression of citizenship in the United States to conclude that the present state of civic engagement is "defensive rather than proactive," describing an individual who "is not an absentee citizen but watchful, even while he or she is doing something else" (p. 311). This cognitive multitasking, which embeds somewhere in its complex webs of information-overload management the notion of civic duty, contributes to a citizenship state best described as *monitorial.* Schudson's (1998) monitorial citizens understand civic duty as predominantly monitorial obligation, stemming from the necessity to remain informed so as to be able to contribute intelligently in public administration, mostly in the event of a crisis. They "scan (rather than read) the informational environment . . . so that they may be alerted on a variety of issues . . . and may be mobilized around those issues in a large variety of ways" (p. 310). Monitorial citizens are capable of action, but they are also calculative of the risk associated with political action.

This monitorial conceptualization is compatible with the principal framework of risk societies (Bauman, 2000, 2005; Beck, 1992; Giddens, 1990), in which individuals are required to balance the conflicting processes of "globalization, individualization, gender revolution, underemployment and global risks." This Beck (1999) terms not post-modernity, but *a second modernity,* in which citizens evaluate actions in the context of perceived risk judged from the perspective of *institutionalized individualism,* that is, institutionalized self-interest (p. 2). For Beck, risk is an outcome of modernity's fascination with control, and, as derivative of cultural perceptions and definitions of frequently socially manufactured uncertainties, it can be managed, by "a peculiar synthesis of knowledge and unawareness" (p. 140). Control of risk lies at the heart of the mythology of technology, which is frequently welcomed for the fantasies of control it sustains. In this context, individuals form their own spheres of *subpolitics,* referring to "politics outside and beyond the representative institutions of the political system of the nation states," and subject to "an (ultimately global) self-organization of politics, which tends to set all areas of society in motion" (p. 39). Schudson (1998) approaches the question of civic responsibility from a different perspective, but he, too, understands the indi-vidualized component of monitorial involvement as a long-term survival strategy for citizens striving towards an ideal division of civic labor in contemporary democracies. Thus, his monitorial citizens employ technology to construct a self-determined sphere of subpolitics, which they then monitor with as perfect an under-standing of the uncertainty surrounding them as the ephemera of the situation will allow.

Converged media afford precisely the confluence of information technology, physical and virtual places, and gamut of practices that enable citizens to construct a comprehensive monitor with which to survey subpolitics, or the self-organized hierarchies of socio-cultural, political, and economic priorities. Monitorial activity is thus ever optimized and pluralized through converged technologies, leading to what Bimber (1998) has described as a state of *accelerated pluralism*, wherein "the Internet contributes to the on-going fragmentation of the present system of interest-based group politics and a shift toward a more fluid, issue-based group politics with less institutional coherence" (p. 135). The navigation of public affairs and the business of self-government are made easier by ceaseless reorganization into fragmented yet more easily surveyable compartmentalized spheres of subpolitics. This plural-izing effect also renders democracies more information-rich, as convergent technologies expand and multiply the information base that presents the referential frame for the monitorial citizen. Yet, this informational base is subject to the redactional practices of the monitorial citizen who scans, edits, and reviews from the basis of the self-developed sphere of subpolitics.

The monitorial citizen is neither a better nor a worse servant of democracy than past citizens were. S/he is the receptor of more information, but this information does not render him or her better informed. The monitorial individual is specific to the era that leaves the citizen with no alternative but to be civically enabled through the surveillance of one's own civic environment. While we may not claim with certainty that it is a more effective mode of involvement, we can recognize that the monitorial model is a solitary mode of civic engagement. Monitoring is not a collective activity. It is possible that monitoring possesses the end-goal of practicing democracy for the collective good, and, in that sense, monitorial citizens fulfill some long-term collective goals. Gobetti (1997) understands this modern citizen as deeply isolated, and describes him/her as:

> . . . a moral, rather than a political animal. She is alone with her conscience, first, and her judgment later. She moves into the world not from within the massive walls of a pre-modern household, but from the fragile private world of her interiority. From this lonely, often solipsistic domain she judges her fellow human beings, their words and their deeds. She recognizes some of those words as advancing valid claims, that is, enforceable rights, and she recognizes her duty to respect those claims. Others are thus present in her mind as another "self," or rather, as her own "self" seen from outside. If she plays this game correctly, a long and peaceful state of nature will be her city, her informal public, her "humankind as a system." (p. 130)

The monitorial citizen contains the potential for activity, but spends most of the time in the suspended inactivity of monitoring, typically practiced from a private sphere. This is a citizen who frequently operates in isolation, though not necessarily in loneliness, although the remote connectivity of the monitor does not lend itself to sociability either. This monitorial function is best understood as the labor of contemporary democracy. Like all labor, civic labor has moments of excitement but is also cloaked in frequently mind-numbing routine. In the end, however, the job gets done.

The digital citizen

Digital citizenship is civic responsibility enabled by digital technologies. Digital citizens operate in the tension created between views of technology as democratizing of post-industrial society (e.g., Bell, 1981; Benkler, 2006; Jenkins, 2006a; Kling, 1996; Negroponte, 1998; Rheingold, 1993) and skeptics ambivalent about the ability of digital media to awaken civic habits that have been dormant for some time (e.g., Hague & Loader, 1999; Hill & Hughes, 1998; Jankowski & van Selm, 2000; Jones, 1997a & b; Papacharissi, 2008). Concurrent rhetoric on growing public cynicism and decreasing participation through traditional channels of civic involvement (e.g., Cappella & Jamieson, 1996, 1997; Fallows, 1996; Patterson, 1993, 1996) creates hope that online digital media like the Internet could bring about a resurrection of contemporary citizenship. Jenkins (2006a), for instance, is hopeful that convergent technologies can provide the platform upon which fan, consumer, and citizen identities can coalesce and solidify, enabling the individual to creatively and civically participate in a democratic culture comprised of both popular culture and civic life reference points. As a result, digitally enabled citizens access civic culture by creatively monitoring and remixing news, popular culture, infotainment, and alternative news to create a subjective palette of civic information, thus 'Photoshopping' their way into democracy (Jenkins, 2006a). Similarly, Benkler (2006), among others, is optimistic about the possibility of convergent technologies sustaining a networked public sphere, which could connect transglobal civically inspired deliberation among a variety of actors, networks, and publics.

As a civic agent, the digital citizen is reified through his/her use of digital media, meaning that digital citizens enter the sphere of civic activity through digital media and are both empowered and restricted by their uses of digital media as civic tools. Thus, access to online technology is as binding to digital citizenship as national geography is to citizenship. Inequality of access to online political participation could create new and reinforced, or reproduce existent, inequalities structured around gender, class, and race, but also education, income level, and age (Hill & Hughes, 1988; Mossberger, Tolbert, & McNeal 2007). Inequality of technological literacy could further socially stratify the uses individuals put online digital technologies to. Hargittai (2008) has shown how an individual's sense of wellbeing, combined with socio-economic status, defines the technical and social context within which technological skill is developed, thus leading into the different variety and complexity of technology uses distinct individuals engage in.

Familiarity with the web, ability to access the web for a multiplicity of purposes, and the ability to manipulate web content become status markers and are associated with higher education and income levels, Asian-American and white users, and male over female users, although these latter differences taper off over time (Hargittai, 2008).

For those with access and technological literacy, the Internet provides public space, but does not inherently democratize or suggest a sense of civic purpose. Online discussions are often dominated by elites and seldom extend to the offline sphere of interaction (Jankowski & van Selm, 2000). Digitally enabled civic activity has not been associated with an increase in political participation or civic engagement (Bimber, 2001), nor has it been identified as a factor in reducing voter cynicism and apathy (Kaid, 2002). Frequently, entertainment uses of the Internet prevail over more informational ones, and do not generate substantial social capital (Althaus & Tewksbury, 2000; Shah, Kwak, & Holbert, 2001). Digital citizens engage in a variety of discussions online, some of which are politically motivated, but that does not always produce offline political impact (Jones, 1997a; Poster, 1995; Schement & Curtis, 1997). Some online civic discussions connect remotely located citizens, while some further isolate them by fragmentizing discussion or further emphasizing insurmountable differences (e.g., Mitra, 1997a & b; Schmitz, 1997). Commercial imperatives occasionally confuse civic objectives, as individuals may have trouble finding political space in net-based locales that resemble networked shopping arcades. Moreover, the Internet is a mass medium, and thus susceptible to the same type of control and commercial concerns that normalize the content of traditional media (Davis, 1999; Margolis, Resnick, & Tu, 1997), thus reinforcing, rather than challenging, the existing political culture (Margolis, Resnick, & Tu, 1997; McChesney, 1995).

At the same time, citizens are increasingly drawn to digital media, and are attracted mostly to interest group and non-partisan websites (Cornfield, Rainie, & Horrigan, 2003). They turn to the web, but for online versions of major media outlets or, for information on public affairs, to net-based news organizations (Kohut,

2003). They enjoy participating in online polls and circulating political jokes and cartoons, but are not drawn to conventional formats of political content online, such as news releases and endorsements (Cornfield, 2004; Cornfield, Rainie, & Horrigan, 2003). Online users who attend or participate in web deliberative groups develop a greater argument repertoire, thus deepening political knowledge (Cappella, Price, & Nir, 2002, p. 73). Face-to-face conversations and online political interactions influence how digital citizens make sense of online news, and whether and how they become politically active (Hardy & Scheufele, 2005). The effect of the Internet as an independent factor is frequently moderated by past and present civic habits that the individual sustains (Jennings & Zeitner, 2003), thus revealing a modest and integrative, rather than radical, impact for digital media upon the routines of the digital citizen.

Often, civic activities that the digitally enabled citizen delves into are campaign-driven, leading to a cultivated array of civic habits and producing a citizen model that is managed (Howard, 2006). Citizens navigate an information market that is simultaneously concentrated by the need of campaigns to manage information and decentralized by citizen web-based communication. The resulting information sphere possesses the ability to inform, involve, connect, and potentially mobilize (Foot & Schneider, 2006). Within this market, information moves quickly along networks in a multi-step flow that involves elites, opinion leaders, and the public in a decentralized and *heterarchical* manner, allowing citizens "the power to have [their] interests represented without acting as a traditional citizenry" (Howard, 2006, p. 187). Howard suggests that contemporary citizenship roles are characterized by thin, shadow, and private modalities. Citizen obligations are thinned because technology alleviates the burden of seeking information and expressing opinion. Rather, convergent technologies favor the opinionated over the informed citizen, by providing the former with multiple networked platforms over which opinion can be expressed, and the latter with simplified civic participation options (polls, signing petitions) that do not require extensive contemplation of civic affairs. Thin citizen habits are enhanced by convergent technologies that track citizen data or digital shadows, thus further customizing the menu of representative options available to digitally enabled thin citizens. Finally, these citizens are private, both in terms of civic reification that is enabled by private, not civic institutions, and by virtue of the private civic habitats they occupy.

Overall, evidence regarding whether convergent technologies support traditional forms of civic engagement is mixed. Individuals do not seem to intuitively put online technologies to use so as to ably fulfill their civic duties, as those are prescribed by preceding models of civic involvement. Conversely, evidence of convergent technologies supporting uses indicative of newer or remediated political habits is extensive, revealing digital citizens who are more interested in combining popular-culture pursuits with political conversation. Subsequently, civic activity is mostly motivated by intrigue over direct democracy features of convergent technologies, rather than specific goal-oriented purposes. Contemporary democracies, however, have not adjusted to these newly developing habits, which do not fit neatly into the structure of democratic institutions, the function of media campaigns, or the traditions of political information dissemination. Our collective definitions of citizenship frequently discount these uses of technology as too frivolous or entertainment-oriented to be truly civic. As Melucci (1994) has argued, "the ceaseless flow of messages only acquires meaning through the codes that order the flux and allow its meanings to be read" (p. 102), and emerging civic expressions may be decoded or interpreted out of context. Within the dominant representative democracy models of later modernity, direct digital democracy features are not expected, cannot be formally absorbed, and thus their occasional integration into mainstream political processes, while successful, is either of a makeshift nature or accidental.

The liquid citizen: a combined model of flexible citizenship

Emerging citizenship modalities have outgrown the civic Republican mold of citizenship and occupy cosmopolitan socio-cultural territory beyond the liberal and neoliberal prescription.

Citizenship is still defined by geographic location, but the civic duties that make a (good) citizen span beyond the spatial confines of citizenship locality (Dahrendorf, 1994; Habermas, 1994). For most individuals, citizenship status is determined by the country in which they were born. As our lives become more mobile and global, an increasing number of individuals find themselves claiming dual citizenship, to include their country of origin and their country of current or permanent residence. Evolving beyond the frame of dual citizenship, individuals have the opportunity to make claims to multinational citizenships throughout the course of their lives, depending on where they choose to work, marry, own property, live, and consume. As Robbins (1998) suggests, individuals are "connected to all sorts of places, causally if not always consciously, including many that we have never traveled to, that we have perhaps only seen on television, including the place where the television itself was manufactured" (p. 1). Civic connections to place are also rhetorically mediated by broadcasting cultures, which solidify a sense of belonging via the dominant media practices of the nation-states. As a result, viewers of the British Broadcasting Corporation, audiences of National Public Radio, or users accessing nationally produced content broadcast online all have the opportunity of diasporically uniting around their nation-home cultures (Morley, 2000).

Nation-states lay claim to the civic identity of an individual, and, conversely, the individual develops a sense of duty towards many global or local, socio-cultural, political, and economic entities beyond the realm of nation-states. Civic identity is no longer fixed in the way it was for our ancestors. The conditions of modernity and late modernity, which enable mobility, financial autonomy, transnational workplaces, and cultural versatility, allow individuals to develop civic bonds with a number of constituencies. These not only evolve and develop as our lives move on, but also constantly transform themselves, driven by the same reflexivity that drives our own existence. It is within these fleeting moments of civic engagement with a variety of civically oriented transnational environments that we experience the cursory glee of citizenship, or what Ong (1999) termed, *a momentary glow of fraternity* (p. 55). And there remain, of course, the excluded: cultural refugees who still long to be included in cultures of citizenship, but who are variably marginalized depending on the global balance between capital and cultural identity.

This reflexivity suggests that we should not only cease to conceive of citizenship as a static process, but also readjust its perimeter. Marshall's typology of citizenship (in Marshall & Bottomore, 1992) distinguished between the civil, political, and social aspects of citizenship: civil referring to equality of civil rights, political defining the legally enforced obligations of citizens, and social describing the objectives of the social welfare state. However, as individuals assume lifestyles that fluidly transfer them through a variety of locations and/or require that they develop everyday interactional routines with individuals and organizations around the world, the conceptual periphery of civil, political, and social is remapped. The task then becomes, for scholars and citizens, that of reconciling civil, political, and social citizenship into a single and coherent civic narrative that captures the role of the contemporary citizen (Fraser & Gordon, 1994).

What are the parameters of this narrative, which combines consumer, cultural, cosmopolitan, monitorial, and digital tropes of civic behaviors? First, the boundaries separating activities that are distinctly political, social, or civic are blurred into subpolitics. Contemporary social movements simultaneously politicize and depoliticize all aspects of public and private life, ultimately rendering determination of what *is* political subjective, and, thus, individually arbitrary. Second, the same spheres of civic, political, and social activity expand to include newer activities that possess civic merit. Several of these reside in the cultural domain, reflecting subcultural, culture-specific, and intercultural practices that shape and modify individual citizen identity. These overlapping, occasionally conflicting, and sometimes parallel spheres of activity can be understood as the *zones of new sovereignty*, representing "mutations in the ways in which localized political and social organizations set the terms and are constitutive of a domain of social existence" (Ong, 1999, p. 215). Convergent modes of economic production and consumption reorganize activities that were exclusive to the sphere of commerce, the social, and the polity into one publicly private and privately public transnational domain, where the flow of civic issues and problems is endless, the tools with which to manage this flow are abundant, but the citizen is potentially confused.

The confusion is a result of the fluidity articulated by these zones of new sovereignty, which, on the one hand, grant individual autonomy generously, but, on the other hand, lack the stability of previous civic environments that enframed this autonomy within a fixed geo-political and socio-cultural context. Free to roam the world and potentially empowered by convergent digital technologies, this citizen has no option but to function as monitorial. Admittedly, to monitor this vast environment is no small task, especially considering that our politically semi-active civic ancestors did a lot less without having to work as much we do. What makes this citizen unique, however, is not the monitorial ability, but, rather, a complex network of abilities and states of involvement the citizen traverses through. These states may be articulated in paradoxical formulation to each other, meaning that they suggest antithetical states of being, thus, potentially, compounding one another and/ or canceling each other out. For instance, the monitorial citizen is simultaneously monitor and voyeur, as the dominant cultures of political infotainment blend information that satisfies the vigilant eye of the civically responsible monitor, as well as the inherent curiosity of the voyeur. Civic uses of convergent media are, simultaneously or adversely, participatory and passive. Some uses of online activism present the pinnacle of collectivity; other introspective civic uses of online media are most effective when pursued in isolation. On a global level, citizens develop affiliations that bind them to both global and local identities, frequently causing them to develop identity narratives that are compatible with a variety of cultures. Is this possible without sacrificing some cultural depth or placing potentially conflicting identities at odds? Finally, political culture blends with consumer culture to produce a menu of civic options that hail audiences as publics of consumers and to be consumed, rendering the distinction between the two "momentary and ephemeral, and always conditional" (Bauman, 2005, p. 10).

Simply put, as citizens of the twenty-first century, we are afforded singular autonomy. This autonomy is the result of the civic demands of our ancestors and the reflexive environment of late modernity. Autonomy is further enhanced by the affordances of convergent technologies, which potentially expand platforms for interaction, avenues for self-expression, and choices and control available to individuals. Autonomy implies self-determination, self-governance, and dependence on the self – all qualities that derive from a strong sense of identity. In a reflexive society, where identity is developed as the conjoined narrative of consecutive choices or reflexes, the anchor of this autonomy is constantly shifted. Liquid living, Bauman (2005) suggests, means "constant self-scrutiny, self-critique and self-censure. Liquid life feeds on the self's dissatisfaction with *itself*" (p. 11). In this sense, the citizen leading a liquid life, this liquid citizen of grand autonomy and flexible context, is a deeply and constantly dissatisfied citizen: a citizen who has been granted limitless autonomy, on the condition that this autonomy not be grounded. Not grounded in specific practices, but, rather, in an ever-evolving amalgamation of everything, the liquid citizen functions in a flexible environment, a civic *flâneur* in a system that has granted autonomy, but has not had time to put the institutional foundations of autonomy in place before the context shifts again. So, digitally equipped, monitorial and voyeuristic, motivated and apathetic, the liquid citizen flows in a fragmented continuum but does not anchor. But this citizen, defined here in abstract terms, has specific habits and routines, some remediations of past political consciousness and some expressions of a new political consciousness emerging. In the next two chapters, old and new habits of the citizen are reviewed, and the flexible theoretical context in which they come to be is presented.

5

The Public Sphere, Expired?
On the democratizing potential of
convergent technologies

To some, the Internet with a capital "I," refers to a series of globally interconnected computers, accessible to the public, which transmit data across networks of networks. The internet with a small "I" describes the technology that enables a variety of applications, systems, and modes and means of communication, which become available to individuals via the technologically networked infrastructure. Perhaps it makes sense to not capitalize the Internet, as, surely, we do not ascribe other media similar grandeur, nor do we refer to such media as *the* Television, *the* Newspaper, or *the* Radio. Still, when discussing the (I)nternet, we frequently employ language evocative of place, geographical or virtual, thus sustaining the ever-present metaphor of the Internet as an alternate space, reality, or experience. Via the use of spontaneous and calculated vernacular, the Internet becomes more than a medium; it is perceived as space, and, in particular, a place that we have in common, as described by the Greek *topos*. Beyond describing a space that individuals have in common, *topos* is frequently employed to also communicate affiliation, belonging, and an emotional connection. In the Aristotelian use of the term, the plural form *topoi* is used to present several suggestions, proposed arguments, or premises up for debate. So the term carries connotations that allow us to understand and interpret the multidimensional meaning of place as a fixed location, but one that carries the opinions, arguments, and expectations of those who reside within its fluid premises.

Convergent technologies, including and built around the Internet, render spaces or *topoi*. As *topos*, the Internet proposes particular uses and activities, or, as Lefebvre (1974/1991) argues, it functions as "a medium of far-off possibilities, as the locus of potentiality" (p. 174). The question, in this chapter, is to what extent do civic uses of the Internet convey *the political*? Do these uses and activities carry civic merit? What is the civic import of proposed political uses of the Internet for the individual and for the polity?

One way, possibly the most obvious, to organize thoughts and respond to these questions is by employing the theoretical model of the public sphere. The reader must understand that the public sphere is not proposed as the ideal model for understanding the political significance of the Internet. Since the beginning of democracy, individuals have strived to convene politically within the locus of a public sphere with more or less success. Thus, this is used as a model that allows us to organize, characterize, and evaluate the merit of civic uses of the Internet. It is possible that the public sphere will emerge as the model that best fits the civic character of the Internet, or that we must adopt a revised or radically new model. At the present time, however, Habermas' public sphere presents a theoretical model that allows us to discuss the civic *gravitas* of the Internet, contextualize it within the contemporary socio-economic setting, and compare it to that of other media.

The public sphere in contemporary democracies

It is not uncommon for scholars to rely on the concept of the public sphere, when seeking to theorize on the democratizing potential of new media (Malina, 1999; Papacharissi, 2002c; Poster, 1995; Sassi, 2000). As a concept, it sets a standard for civic involvement within representative democracy. It also presents a primal form of human civic instinct, expressed through the need to convene and confer within democratic contexts. Conceptualized formally by Jürgen Habermas (1962/1989), the public sphere has always served as the domain of social life where public opinion is expressed by means of rational public discourse and debate. Based on Kantian emphasis on the use of reason in public debate, it is where citizens go to analyze, discuss, or argue about public affairs. Habermas traces the progression of the public sphere from the Athenian agora of Ancient Greece, to that of the Roman

Republic, to britannic coffeehouses and French literary salons of the eighteenth and nineteenth centuries. The path of the public sphere has been shaped by historical conditions that have similarly transformed the distinction between public and private spaces, the relation of technology to communication and society, and the civic trajectory of citizenship. But it must be understood that the public sphere is an abstraction that can materialize in a loud, smoke-filled coffeehouse, an orderly Parliament environment, or a crowded street market. The setting may be more or less formal, the circumstances contrived or spontaneous, and the make-up of the public inclusive or elitist. The common theme lies in the rationally structured, common-good-focused, discussion of public affairs.

The public sphere in a representative democracy is where citizens deliberate and debate on public affairs, with public accord and decision-making as implied common goals. Habermas describes it thus "a sphere which mediates between society and state, in which the public organizes itself as the bearer of public opinion, accords with the principle of the public sphere, that principle of public information which once had to be fought for against the arcane politics of monarchies and which since that time has made possible the democratic control of state activities" (Habermas, 1973, p. 351). The ultimate goal is public accord and decision-making, although these goals may not necessarily be achieved routinely. The value of the public sphere lies in its ability to facilitate uninhibited and diverse discussion of public affairs, thus reifying and reproducing democratic traditions and enabling citizens to directly interact within a representative political system. Within a representative democracy, the public sphere serves to inject the system with a healthy dose of direct communication and debate. In the absence of a robust public sphere, it is possible that citizens may feel the distance between them and their elected representatives, which may then translate into feelings of detachment, apathy, and cynicism. A vigorous public sphere helps citizens remain plugged into the daily routines of democratic governance and public affairs. I argue that several civic uses of the Internet develop in yearning for a long-lost public sphere. These last two chapters explain how these civic uses come to be.

The public sphere ideally facilitates rational discourse of public affairs directed towards the common good, and operates autonomously from the state and/or the economy (Garnham, 1990; Habermas, 1973). This autonomy is compromised in the modern era, according to Habermas, as the public sphere is colonized by the rhetoric of commercialization and corporate agendas. Thus, the discourse produced is dominated by and furthers the objectives of advertising and public relations. Habermas finds that, in contemporary democracies, the public sphere becomes a vehicle for capitalist hegemony and ideological reproduction. Thus, public life is disrupted by permeating imperatives of commodification, which interfere with transparency of process and rationality of deliberation. The media, in particular, central in supporting democracy through public service, have actually corrupted the processes of public thought, deliberation, opinion, and action (Keane, 1991; Robbins, 1993).

The public sphere involves the public, employs public space, hosts discussions of public affairs, and generates public opinion, but is conceptually distinct from any of those four concepts, equally important for students and observers of politics. The public sphere must not be confused with public space. While public space provides the expanse that allows the public sphere to convene, it does not guarantee a healthy public sphere. The public sphere also serves as a forum for, but is conceptually distinct from, the public, public affairs, or public opinion. According to Habermas (1962/1989), "public opinion can only come into existence when a reasoning public is presupposed," and that is what distinguishes it from individuals expressing mere opinions, or mere opinions about public affairs, opinions expressed within simple proceedings that are made public, or a public consisting of individuals who assemble. Because, according to Habermas, the public sphere has been compromised to the point where its actual existence is in doubt, it is best understood as a metaphor. It is also possible for political activity or discussion to carry civic merit, but exist outside the conceptual locus of the public sphere. I emphasize this point, for, as we examine political tendencies online, it becomes apparent that, while some aspire to the public sphere ideal, several contribute civically, but via a *modus operandi* conceptually divorced from the public sphere ideal.

Prior to examining how the Internet fits the public sphere model, however, it is essential to consider how other media have interacted with the public sphere. Within the liberal model of the public sphere, mass media play a critical part in informing and directing public opinion, especially since mass society simultaneously abridges gender/class/race borders and renders direct communication among varying public constituencies more difficult. It is Habermas' argument that the commercialized mass media have turned the public sphere into a space where the rhetoric and objectives of public relations and advertising are prioritized. Commercial interests, a capitalist economy, and mainstream media content have colonized the public sphere and compromised rational and democratic public discourse, with television frequently playing a vanguard role (Habermas, 2004).

With the public sphere in this compromised state, the mass media play a critical part in informing and directing public opinion. This point of view resonates with leading communication scholars, who connect the erosion of public culture with the objectives of commercial media (e.g., Carey, 1995; Putnam, 1996), and find that commercial media "supersaturate viewers with political information," and that, as a result, "this tumult creates in viewers a sense of activity rather than genuine civic involvement" (Hart, 1994, p. 109).

Additional conditions associated with the transcendence to industrial, post-industrial modern and post-modern society contribute to a deteriorating public sphere and declining interest in politics. For instance, in contemporary representative models of democracy, politicians, opinion leaders, and the media frequently rely on aggregations of public opinion obtained through polls, as opposed to the rational exchange of opinions fostered by the public sphere. Jacques Derrida (1992) terms this abstraction of public opinion, routinely evoked by politicians and the media in appealing to the public sentiment, the "silhouette of a phantom, the haunting fear of a democratic consciousness" (p. 84). From a different perspective, Herbst's (1993) "numbered voices" point to the substitution of individual and detailed personal opinion on public affairs with a concentration of viewpoints usually expressed in the bipolarity of the yes/no polling response format. Thus, deliberation of public affairs within the public sphere is postponed as citizens are called upon to express agreement or disagreement with pre-scribed options. Research also indicates that this simplification of complex political issues leads to misinformation and growing civic skepticism. The media frequently employ frames that prioritize politicizing an issue rather than encouraging rational deliberation of it (Fallows, 1996; Patterson, 1993). As the prospect of civic par-ticipation is deemphasized and skepticism is reinforced through negative or cynical coverage in the mass media, growing cynicism spreads in a spiraling manner (Cappella & Jamieson, 1996, 1997), thus further alienating citizens from the prospect of civic activity.

Several scholars disagree with the public sphere model, for they find that it overestimates civic engagement in past societies and civilizations. Inclusion in the public sphere is a privilege that most citizens of past democracies did not enjoy. In the Greek and Roman republics, participation in the public sphere was not afforded to those who were not considered citizens, and women, slaves, and non-property-owners were excluded. Similarly, later incarnations of the public sphere were structured around privi-lege, special interests, or the elite. The notion of exclusion from the public sphere is present in Fraser (1992), who suggested that Habermas' examples of past, romanticized public spheres excluded women and non-propertied classes, and proposed a post-industrial model of co-existing public spheres or counter-publics, which form in response to their exclusion from the dominant sphere of debate. These multiple public spheres, though not equally powerful, articulate, or privileged, exist to give voice to collective identities and interests. Schudson's (1998) historical review of past political activity further questioned the actual exist-ence of a public sphere, and argued that public discourse is not the main ingredient of democracy. Robbins (1993) suggested that the mythic town square that the public sphere model is based on is nothing more than an imagined characterization of public space, or a "phantasmagoria: an agora . . . that is only a phantasm" (p. 7).

In the same vein, Keenan (1993) interpreted the public sphere as something that is always "structurally elsewhere, neither lost nor in need of recovery and rebuilding, but defined by its resistance to being made present" (p. 135). Alternatively, while some recognize the impact of commercialized media on democratic discourse, they also suggest that the media market and the public interest need not be perceived as irreconcilable (Curran, 1991; Mancini, 1991).

Most sites of public discourse do not remain public in their entirety or for eternity, and, therefore, scholars acknowledge the presence of multiple, distinct or overlapping, spaces that operate away from the singularity of a public sphere, yet are better for hosting robust, transnational, and diverse democratic discussions (Morley, 2000; Robbins, 1993). These shifting spaces of public discourse are more hospitable to a globalized spectrum of issues, conflicting dogmas of egalitarianism and social justice, and reflexive modes of representation (Fraser, 2008). Cosmopolitan democracies, structured around the nexus of identity politics but obligated to reconcile individualistic and pluralistic priorities, might be better served by more flexible public and private spaces. Thus, our operationalization of the public sphere construct must also carry a practical foundation, which should specify how these dilemmas of late modernity can be resolved (Dahlgren, 1991).

To this end, many scholars find that the public sphere model places undue emphasis on consensus as a requirement for a healthy democracy. For instance, Lyotard (1984) argued that Habermas overemphasized rational accord as a condition for a democratic public sphere, and insisted that it is anarchy, individuality, and disagreement that have had and can lead, to genuine democratic emancipation. Lyotard's dissent was founded in Derrida's (1997) deconstructivist approach, which emphasized undecidability as the necessary constant in any form of public deliberation. The deconstructivist emphasis on dissent is more inclusive of multiple forms of political discussion, beyond the rationally guided debate. It is unclear whether Habermas himself intended for rationality to be understood this rigidly, for he has clarified that his work is frequently misread to this end (Habermas, 2004). Regardless of this, the focus on discord and anarchy helps broaden the theoretical scope of what we could term *democratic discourse*, and allows the inclusion of several breeds of political discussion present online.

Mouffe (2000, 2005) explicitly connected these ideas to contemporary, pluralist democracy and posed the concept of agonistic pluralism as a more realistic alternative to the public sphere. Mouffe's (2000) critique is based on the impossibility of true plurality within a modern or post-modern deliberative democracy. Thus, she proposed agonistic pluralism, as a "vibrant clash of democratic political positions," guided by undecidability, and more receptive than the deliberative model to the plurality of voices that develop within contemporary pluralist societies (p. 104). Specifically, the "'agonistic' approach acknowledges the real nature of its frontiers and the forms of exclusion that they entail, instead of trying to disguise them under the veil of rationality or morality" (p. 105). Mouffe's (2000, 2005) emphasis on the agonistic foreshadows modes of political expression that have been popularized through the Internet, including blogging, YouTube's privately produced content, and discussion on online political boards.

It becomes apparent that the public sphere is most meaningful as a metaphor that, when materialized, may take on several shapes and forms. It is possible that, through the multiple incarnations of the public sphere, the original ideal and metaphor become confused. The metaphor itself, as theorized by Habermas, has been broadened to address contemporary critique and approaches (Habermas, 1992). What remains to be seen is how well, how poorly, or simply how the Internet fits this metaphor. Within this context, online media, including the Internet, could host a virtual sphere or revitalize the public sphere.

Conversations on the democratizing potential of online convergent technologies are usually evocative of the mythos surrounding the new, and thus fueled by utopian euphoria on the transformative potential of newer technologies, as well as dystopic apprehension. Those more optimistic perceive them as democratizing forces (e.g., Bell, 1981; Johnson & Kaye, 1998; Kling, 1996; Negroponte, 1998; Rheingold, 1993), while moderates emphasize the pluralizing effect of online technologies (e.g., Bimber, 1998; Blumler & Gurevitch, 2001), and skeptics question the impact of these technologies on civic deliberation (e.g., Bimber & Davis, 2003; Davis, 1999; Hill & Hughes, 1998; Jankowski & van Selm, 2000; Jones, 1997a; Margolis & Resnick, 2000; Scheufele & Nisbet, 2002). Most, however, tend to assess the democratizing potential of online convergent technologies against the following three criteria, as they directly affect the social and political capital generated by online media: *access* to information, *reciprocity* of communication, and *commercialization* of online space (e.g., Malina, 1999; Papacharissi, 2002c; Sassi, 2000).

Access to information

Rational discussion and structured arguments presuppose access to information, as it is information that provides the basis and evidence upon which solid arguments rest. It would seem that by enabling greater access to more information, net-related technologies would at least provide citizens with the tools with which to develop informed viewpoints and engage in substantive political discussions. Keeping in mind the narrow agendas frequently set by mainstream media, it would be reasonable to expect that a fluid medium like the Internet supports a greater variety of issue agendas and information access points. What does not necessarily follow is that merely greater *access* to information, enabled by online media, will directly lead to increases in political participation, greater civic engagement, or trust in the political process (Bimber, 2001; Kaid, 2002). There are several reasons why.

First, the advantages of the Internet as an information gateway can be enjoyed only by those few who have access to it (Pavlik, 1994; Sassi, 2005; Williams & Pavlik, 1994). With global digital diffusion presently at 24% (Africa: 6.8%; Asia: 19.4%; Europe: 52%; Latin America / Caribbean: 30%; Middle East: 28%; North America: 75%; Oceania/Australia: 60% – World Internet Usage Statistics, www.internetworldstats.com/stats.htm, accessed December 2009), it might be more appropriate to discuss local, regional, or national public spheres rather than a global public sphere. Second, while digitally enabling citizens (Abramson, Arterton, & Orren, 1988; Grossman, 1995; Jones, 1997a; Rash, 1997), online media simultaneously reproduce class, gender, and race inequalities of the offline public sphere (DiMaggio, Hargittai, Celeste, & Shafer, 2004; Hill & Hughes, 1998). Even though the medium allows global connections, individuals typically employ it to connect to those they already know from offline points of contact, however geographically dispersed those points of contact may be (e.g., Hargittai, 2007; Papacharissi, 2008). Finally, the information access the Internet provides also typically invites entertainment uses of the medium (Althaus & Tewksbury, 2000; Shah, Kwak, & Holbert, 2001), the public sphere relevance of which is arguable (Dahlgren, 2005; Moy, Manosevitch, Stamm, & Dunsmore, 2005). Increased access to information does not ensure that the content accessed will be diverse.

Access enabled by net-related technologies spans beyond access to information, and may include greater access to groups, persons, organizations, and elites that are frequently bearers of information and opinion leaders. This type of access is multidirectional, allowing parties to connect more easily with each other. For instance, access can include connecting to political elites that shape the public agenda, and the ability for these elites to communicate directly with the electorate. Thus, in addition to enabling access to information, online media make it possible for privately motivated individuals and groups to challenge the public agenda (e.g., Grossman, 1995; Rash, 1997), connect the government to citizens (Arterton, 1987), and allow for two-way communication through interactive features (e.g., Abramson, Arterton, & Orren, 1988). Still, greater access to information and communication channels does not ensure increases in civic engagement. Online political conversations can be as easily dominated by elites as offline ones. Access to information does not guarantee that information will be accessed. Similarly, access to information does not render an electorate more active or efficacious.

Reciprocity

Online media enable conversations that can transcend geographic boundaries. They also allow for relative anonymity in personal expression, which could lead to empowered and uninhibited public opinion. Still, the technological potential for global communication does not oblige people from different cultural backgrounds to also become more understanding of each other's differences (e.g., Hill & Hughes, 1998). Reciprocity in communication necessitates that both parties are involved equally in mutual conversation. Reciprocity in conversation also implies a mutual exchange of opinion and information, wherein the same advantages and privileges are granted and observed by all participants. A reciprocal deliberative model may be either globalized or tribalized, based on the motivations of the political actors that put it to use. Several scholars argue that, in order for online discussions to be democratizing, they must involve two-directional communication, cover topics of common interest, and be motivated by a mutually shared commitment to rational and focused discourse. These elements afford online conversations a degree of *reciprocity*, which can truly help connect citizens of democracies, rather than reproducing fragmented spheres of conversation.

Specifically, online discussion of public affairs can connect citizens sharing similar motivations but may also reproduce and magnify cultural disparities (e.g., Mitra, 1997a & b; Schmitz, 1997). Scholars routinely point to online political discussions that are too amorphous, fragmented, dominated by a few, and too specific to live up to the Habermasian ideal of rational accord. In fact, many discussions online transpire in the form of corresponding posts, which enable opinion-expression, but do not necessarily engender conversation. The medium tends to favor information-gathering practices that are of a thin, shadow, and private nature (Howard, 2006). However, discussion, and, in particular, public-sphere-specific discourse, require reciprocity, in order to flourish. While relative anonymity enables political expression online (Akdeniz, 2002), that expression does not always result in discussion of greater substance or political impact (Jones, 1997a; Poster, 1995; Schement & Curtis, 1997). It should also be noted that online communication typically takes place among people who already know each other offline (Uslaner, 2004), thus connecting already-existing spheres of contact. These frequently include elites, or are dominated by elites, producing discussions that do not always tran-scend into political action (Jankowski & van Selm, 2000). Other analysis of online political deliberation reveals that collective use of the Internet can lead to greater political participation, but only when it is characterized by trust and reciprocity (e.g., Kobayashi, Ikeda, & Miyata, 2006). Yet studies examining the connection between online political talk and social capital find that the social connections people make online do not necessarily promote trust; on the contrary, evidence suggests that online forums frequently bring together mistrusting people (Uslaner, 2004). So, a confused and confusing public valuing reciprocity in conversation, but not interested in exercising it in online communication, becomes polit-ically engaged online, but to varying degrees and with arguable political consequences.

Commercialization

Finally, *commercialization* presents a primary concern for research-ers who examine the potential of the virtual sphere. The Internet has gradually transitioned into an online multi-shopping mall and less of a deliberative space, which influences the orientation of digital political discussion. Even though these commercial uses run contrary to the architecturally open and public-service-oriented structure of the net, markets frequently employ traditional media commodity logic in commercial appropriations of net-based platforms (Locke, Levine, Searls, & Weinberger, 2001). As a medium constructed within a capitalist context, the Internet is susceptible to the profit-making impulses of the market, which do not traditionally prioritize civic participation or democratization (O'Loughlin 2001; Schiller, 2000, 2006). While equipped with an open architecture that resists commercialization (Lessig, 2005) it is not immune to commercial objectives (McChesney, 1995; Newhagen & Rafaeli, 1996). For instance, in a study of how an online democracy project measured up to the public sphere ideal, Dahlberg (2001) demonstrated how such initiatives, while partially successful, ultimately are unable to attract a sizable portion of the population and are frequently "marginalized by commercial sites, virtual communities of common interest, and liberal individualist political practices" (p. 615). Employing the Habermasian concepts of colonization and juridification, Salter (2005) showed how mainstream legal tendencies may restrict the democratizing potential of the Internet. More importantly, the Internet is unable to single-handedly "produce political culture when it does not exist in society at large" (McChesney, 1995, p. 13). Scholars also argue that the content featured online has yet to become distinct from that provided by traditional mass media or to draw in the average citizen in the manner in which traditional media do (Bimber & Davis, 2003; Margolis, Resnick, & Tu, 1997; Scheufele & Nisbet, 2002).

Finally, through collaboration and mergers with media conglomerates, creative factions of the Internet are colonized by the commercial concerns that standardize the content of traditional media (Davis, 1999; Margolis, Resnick, & Tu, 1997). Despite the anti-commodity nature of open source protocols, most theory on the information society seems to suggest a proliferation of a globally networked culture of commodification (Hassan, 2008). These tendencies do not inherently transform the Internet, in its entirety, into a commercial sphere. The commercial nature of the Internet, however, co-exists with its public interest roots by following rules that are unique and have little to do with the commercialization of other media. These singular elements point to the Internet as a commercially public medium, and this hybrid mode of functioning and self-sustaining puts forward hybrid public spaces, in which new civic habits are formed. These more recent civic routines are examined in the chapter to follow.

Scholarly examinations of the Internet as a public sphere all point to the conclusion that online digital technologies create a public space, but do not inevitably enable a public sphere. Research so far has shown that *access* to information, *reciprocity* of communication, and *commercialization* are the three primary conditions that prohibit the transition from public space to public sphere. A new public space is not synonymous with a new public sphere, in that a virtual space simply enhances discussion; a virtual sphere should enhance democracy. This need not be interpreted as a predicament or a failure. It is not online technologies that fail the public sphere test – rather, it could be the other way around. This does not necessarily suggest a failure of the online political apparatus; it could merely suggest that the language we use to describe online technologies routinely underestimates their potential. Neither are the concepts we use flawed; nor is the civic nature of the medium. The fit, however, between the two, is not ideal, which is why it becomes necessary to consider alternative ways of explicating the civic character of net-related technologies. As individuals become more comfortable with online media, newer appropriations of the Internet suggest singular trends that locate civic activity away from the public sphere ideal in a direction that may be meaningful, but not what we may have experienced in our civic past. These trends articulate the democratizing potential of the Internet in a way that has little in common with the Habermasian public sphere but more in common with contemporary public impulses and desires. Moreover, these trends demarcate the profile of an increasingly more flexible or liquid citizen who functions with greater autonomy in contexts more fluid than those delineated by the public sphere. Let me be more specific.

A new kind of public

In writing about the ambient omnipresence of media in public spaces, and the ways in which they interrupt and re-organize our daily routines, Anna McCarthy (2001) wrote:

> . . . Public spaces are not purely and self-evidently public; they are, like every other cultural space, characterized by particular configurations of public and private. Indeed, what makes the public/private division such a major category of social power is the fact that it is dynamic and flexible, varying from place to place. Taking this into account allows us to specify, with a great deal of precision, how the visual and bodily constitution of the subject as a citizen, of a consumer, or a trespasser occurs in quantum ways within the spaces of everyday life. (p. 121)

It becomes evident that several of the abstractions against which we evaluate our civic adequacy as citizens are quite elusive. The public/private dichotomy is historically sensitive and constantly redefined; the public sphere presents a metaphor evoked more often to inspire, rather than describe, actual incarnations of good citizenship; citizenship itself is an abstract, subject to the dominant ideologies of the eras within which the right to citizenship is exercised.

Earlier in this volume, the public/private binary was explicated so as to afford an understanding of how categorizations of space suggest and reflect civic identities and activities of an era. In late modern democracies, public and private boundaries are constantly readjusted or blurred, resulting in a privatization of public space and a possible (return to the) home as political space. Thus, it is difficult to identify public spaces that are not associated with the state or with the commercial interest. Concurrently, private spaces are gradually becoming spaces of commercial transaction. As a result, individuals frequently collapse private and public modalities of expression and existence into the realm of the social, constantly and personally readjusting the boundaries of private and public spaces. Convergent technologies further augment these trends by multiplying or pluralizing our spheres of interaction and potential audiences, all the while leaving it up to us to set the boundaries of private and public. Citizenship then traverses these planes of activity across national and transnational domains, in possession of the grandest democratic privilege, autonomy, but with no stable institutional structures to exercise this autonomy against.

The irony of receiving the prize of autonomy at the conclusion of millennia of democratic struggles, and during an era of accelerated reflexivity, is inescapable. What is the meaning of autonomy without the rigidity of institutions that previously stifled it? is autonomy defined, if not as the process of liberating oneself from institutional forces of suppression? I do not suggest that all conditions potentially suppressive of individual autonomy have been eclipsed, but, rather, that they have become increasingly interconnected and malleable, thus simultaneously awarding and complicating individual autonomy. The democratic paradox of seeking autonomy through processes of representative democracy that prioritize majority rule and accord compromises the ideal of plurality (e.g., Mouffe, 2000). The institutionalization of representative democracy at the level of the nation-state runs counter to global tendencies and transnational networks of power, which externally compromise the agendas of nationally elected democratic governments (e.g., Thompson, 1995). The professionalization of politics yields a public that is more skeptical, yet muted out through the processes of aggregate public opinion polling (e.g. Herbst, O'Keefe, Shapiro, Lindeman, & Glynn, 2004). The dominant organizing logic of capitalism casts ancillary economic dimensions over public and private practices that were previously purely civic. Finally, online convergent technologies afford direct democracy features that are difficult to integrate within a globalized society that turns to a system of representation as a way of managing its sheer mass and reach.

Prospects of resurrecting the civic purity of public and private in the face of these growing, and antithetical, tendencies, without highlighting these contradictions even further, are grim. Thompson (1995) instead suggests that we "try to free our way of thinking about public life from the grip of the traditional approach . . . [and] try to refashion our way of thinking about public life at the same time as we reflect on the new kind of publicness created" (p. 245). Doing so may require revisiting language we employ to describe civic practices.

Research and practice indicate that the Internet does not constitute a public or virtual sphere; if anything, it presents less of a democracy than several of the public sphere's past incarnations (Dahlgren, 2005; Noam, 2005). On the other hand, models that emphasize the plurality enabled by digital media (Bimber, 1998), contemporary citizen needs and wants (Schudson, 1998), and the ability of the Internet to amplify political processes (Agre, 2002) present more pragmatic assessments of online media potential. Finally, romanticized retrospectives of civic engagement often distort the affordances of technologies of the present.

Online technologies afford us spaces, public and private, rather than a public sphere. These spaces accommodate a new kind of publicity and privacy, constructed via the amalgamation of private and public interests. Whereas in the past public had been used to demarcate the end of private, and private signaled a departure from public, the terms no longer imply such opposition, especially in terms of how they are architecturally employed for the construction of place. Spaces presented by convergent technologies are hybrid public and private spaces. Furthermore, the extent to which the economic motive differentiates public from private, thus associating the private sector with capitalist and market-oriented imperatives, and public interest with non-commercial public-good-driven agendas, is also challenged. The economies of public and private spaces are of hybrid form. These hybrid economies of space epitomize and legitimize the hybridization of capitalist and public interest objectives, which, in Habermasian analysis, is responsible for the demise of the public sphere itself. Yet they demonstrate that the public sphere may not be the most meaningful lens through which to evaluate the democratizing potential of online technologies. On the contrary, these hybrid economies of space presented by convergent media suggest a collapse of what Castoriadis (1975, 1986) had described as the distinct tropes of the *capitalist* and the *creative* imaginaries.

Castoriadis (1975/1987) understood the creative imaginary as representative of the potential for great autonomy and creativity, the result of cultural density and the richness of the democratic struggles of the eighteenth, nineteenth, and early twentieth centuries. All societies create their imaginaries, in the form of institutions, laws, norms, behaviors, habits, beliefs, and other dominant modalities. However, genuinely autonomous societies are deeply aware of this fact, whereas heteronomous societies tend to attribute this fact to specific external authorities associated with religion or historical circumstance. Thus, members of autonomous societies bear the self-awareness, cynicism, and liberation that stem from the conscious actualization of autonomy. The capitalist imaginary, on the other hand, is emblematic of commercially driven narratives that sustain the closed-ended policies of prevalent economic models. In this regard, Castoriadis (2007) wrote:

> I think that we are at a crossing in the roads of history, history in the grand sense. One road already appears clearly laid out . . . the road of the loss of meaning, of the repetition of empty forms, of conformism, apathy, irresponsibility, and cynicism at the same time as it is that of the tightening grip of the capitalist imaginary of unlimited expansion of "rational mastery,"

pseudorational pseudomastery, of an unlimited expansion of consumption for the sake of consumption, that is to say, for nothing, and of a techno-science that has become autonomized along its path and that is evidently involved in the domination of this capitalist imaginary. The other road should be opened: it is not at all laid out. It can be opened only through a social and political awakening, a resurgence of the project of individual and collective autonomy, that is to say, of the will to freedom. This would require an awakening of the imagination and of the creative imaginary. (p. 146)

These two roads are presented as distinct paths, but not opposite ends of a continuum. It is my argument that the convergent structure of popular new technologies, together with the collapse of public and private boundaries, and the self-actualization of citizenship via non-civic habits, propose a similar collapse of the capitalist and creative imaginaries.

These commercially public spaces may not render a public sphere, but they provide hybrid economies of space where individuals can engage in interaction that is civic, among other things. These spaces are essential in maintaining a politically active consciousness that may, when necessary, articulate a sizable oppositional voice in response to concentrated ownership regulation (as described in McChesney, 2004) or US foreign policy (as described in Hands, 2006). While distinct from the public sphere of the past, these tendencies may present a more accurate reflection of contemporary and post-modern public needs and wants. They do not reside strictly within the creative imaginary, and they are obviously not exclusive to the capitalist imaginary. Yet, they present personal and creative interventions into the logic of the capitalist imaginary, that effectively blend the capitalist and creative imaginaries into a sphere of civic interaction defined by the individual.

Within this individually sketched-out sphere, consisting of spaces that are simultaneously public and private, technologies are employed to sustain narration of an identity that is in constant evolution, or fluid. Structured around a vernacular that is contemporary and accessible (to the technologically literate), these technologies of narration connect atomized civic actions, with all "implications of continuity, yet of 'forgetting' the experience of this continuity" intact (Anderson, 1983, p. 205). Similarly, convergent technologies create a new civic vernacular for anonymous individuals, allowing an actualization of civic identity in tropes distinct from the deliberative model of the public sphere. These tropes are simultaneously evocative and forgetful of the civic past, allowing citizens to acknowledge and move beyond it. New habits comprising this new civic vernacular are explicated next.

6

A Private Sphere

Contemporary civic tendencies are characterized by a variety of atomized actions, taking place in a plurality of spaces that are both public and private. These tendencies are the property of a citizen leading a largely reflexive existence in order to actualize an identity that is fluid. The civic base of this identity is exercised via activity emanating from mostly a monitorial, rather than deliberative or proactive, standpoint. New civic habits enabled and created in response to current interpellations of the creative and capitalist imaginaries serve to create a new civic vernacular for citizens transitioning to a fluidly composed model of citizenship. The common thread among all these tendencies can be located in the individual who operates civically in a political sphere that is founded on the tension between public and private. Participating in a MoveOn.org online protest, expressing political opinion on blogs, viewing or posting content on YouTube, or posting a comment in an online discussion group represents an expression of dissent with a public agenda, determined by mainstream media and political actors. It stands as a private, digitally enabled, intrusion on a public agenda determined by others.

Strikingly, these potentially powerful acts of dissent emanate from a private sphere of interaction, meaning that the citizen engages and is enabled politically through a private media environment located within the individual's personal and private space. This private sphere is rhetorically established by the individual by utilizing existing and imagined geographies of place. Whereas in the truest iterations of democracy the citizen was enabled through the public sphere, in contemporary democracies the citizen becomes politically emancipated via a private sphere of reflection, expression, and behavior. This relocation suggests that we re-examine the spatiality of citizenship. Within this private sphere, the citizen is alone, but not lonely or isolated. The citizen is connected, and operates in a mode and with political language determined by him or her. Operating from a civically *privé* environment, the citizen enters the public spectrum by negotiating aspects of his/her privacy as necessary, depending on the urgency and relevance of particular situations. Primarily still monitorial in orientation, the citizen is able to become an agonist of democracy, if needed, but in an atomized mode. This chapter explicates the model of a private sphere, in search of contemporary metaphors and language with which to assess the democratic nature of online digital media. Previous research and theory, as well as examples or illustrations of digital democracy, are employed to construct and support this model.

The private sphere has been understood in the past as complementary or opposite to the public sphere. Usually associated with the family or the home, the private sphere serves to enforce a conventional and binary opposition between public and private. For several philosophers, especially during the Ancient Greco-Roman period, exclusive pre-occupation with the private sphere serves to nullify man's true nature, which directs primary existence via the public sphere. In modern times, the private sphere is associated with privacy rights and the right to be left alone, but is also viewed as a space where marginalized interests and counter-publics are relegated. Finally, as the public sphere becomes appropriated as commercial terrain, the private sphere emerges as a space seemingly immune to the capitalist imaginary. However, the subsistence of consumption and the ubiquity of media are capable of transferring the agenda of the capitalist imaginary into the home. How is it then that the private sphere can sustain a new civic vernacular through which individual citizens may connect back to publics, counter-publics, and hybrid spheres as they choose?

Heidegger (1962) argued that it is only in the private sphere that one can be one's true, authentic self. The private sphere presents the space where all the potentialities of being may be freely expressed, far from the interpretations of being that may be imposed by the public. Heidegger's work has been critiqued for its abstraction, obscurity, and manipulation of language. However, it is important to understand how the privacy of one's being feeds individual authenticity and self-actualization in ways equally important to enacting behaviors in public. Moreover, as public and private boundaries collapse into the realm of the social, the challenge lies in distinguishing sociality from solitude, as they are practiced in realms public or private.

Earlier in this volume, the effect of electronic technologies on time and space was discussed. Like previous transportation and communication media, telecommunications, broadcasting, convergent digital platforms that combine both older and newer media have a dramatic effect on the relation between time and space, referred to as the *uncoupling of space and time* (Thompson, 1995). Therefore, spatial transportation to public places no longer requires the traversing of temporal and geographical boundaries. Not only are public experiences immediately transmittable to private individuals, but it is possible to experience public events from the privacy of one's personal sphere, providing for the experience of *despatialized simultaneity* (Thompson, 1995). This reorganization of the time–space continuum effected by modern communication media, together with the ability of media to weave cultural landscapes of reference, results in transforming the private sphere of the home into a space that is both public and private (Barnett, 2004). But the private sphere remains in the temporally fixed zone of the home. The mobile capabilities of convergent media enable individuals to simulate the conditions of the private sphere in spatial and temporal terms removed from the fixed locality of the home. Therefore, the private sphere is a sphere inclusive of the home, possibly, but mostly a sphere possessing what Raymond Williams (1974) termed *mobile privatization*, that is, the ability media offer audiences to simultaneously stay home and travel places. The comfort of remaining in the realm of the familiar while at the same time being able to experience the other or the unknown is a capability of the private sphere augmented by online convergent technologies. In the networked private sphere, activities are structured around organizations of space and time determined and conditioned by the individual operating as a private agent. Beyond physical and virtual, the private sphere is rhetorically claimed by the individual and enframed by technology.

There are reasons why the mobile autonomy of the private sphere is particularly harmonious to contemporary modalities of citizenship. First, as political power is still territorially exercised in contexts both local and global, the mobility of the private sphere potentially extends the agency of the private individual but also fragments political discourse (Garnham, 2000). Second, given the informational overload produced by fragmentized or harmonious, cosmopolitan or localized counter-publics, a mobile private sphere enables the frequently monitorial citizen to efficiently balance conflicting and potentially overwhelming civic demands. Finally, a mobile private sphere that functions as the basis of civic emancipation is concordant with values of individualism, autonomy, and self-expression that are prevalent in late modern democracies of developed societies. The mobility of this private sphere further permits that everyday routines be interlaced in ways that render the individual reachable anywhere and anytime, in a way that may "revolutionalize" control of everyday life (Castells, Fernandez-Ardevol, Linchuan Qiu & Sey, 2006; Ling & Donner, 2009). Inglehart and Welzel (2005) conducted a series of studies that comparatively mapped the progression of modernity across cultures of developed and developing societies to conclude that post-industrialization has ratified a transition from existential to self-expression values. Self-expression values are connected to the desire to control one's environment, a stronger desire for autonomy, and the need to question authority. These values are aligned with fantasies of control sustained by online technologies of mobility. Self-expression values are not uncivic, and have frequently led to subversive collective action movements on environmental protection, fair trade, and gender equality. These findings present practical evidence of trends that European schools of philosophy and sociology have outlined since the middle of the twentieth century, using a variety of traditions, terminology, and analytical methods (e.g., Bauman, 2001; Castoriadis, 1986; Giddens, 1990;

Habermas, 2004; Hesse, 1930/1968; Kondylis, 1991; Mouffe, 2000, 2005).

Additional evidence on changing civic textures and evolving democratic values may be located through an examination of social capital and civil society norms in contemporary democracies in flux (Putnam, 2002). In Great Britain, social capital levels have remained the same for the past fifty years; however, subtle changes in how individuals understand and practice collective lives reveal a decline in face-to-face interaction, the ascent of public opinion polling, and the proliferation of issue publics (Hall, 2002). In the United States, declines in social capital have been replaced with new forms that are friendlier to the demands of mobile and professionally oriented lifestyles, but do not minimize disparities between those privileged and those marginalized (Skocpol, 2002; Wuthnow, 2002).

France, far removed from a decline in social capital, is experiencing a reorganization of its own civil society, brought on by immigrant tensions, the emancipation of civil society from the state, and the process of creating new social ties between old and new civic habits and inhabitants (Worms, 2002). Germany is undergoing a similar transformation, with a change in the texture of social capital produced, having to do with a preference for *informal* forms of civic association and a simultaneous proliferation of association networks that are of a hierarchy-free or flat structure (Offe & Fuchs, 2002). Spain is witnessing similar trends and a transition from civil to uncivil, mostly cultural or informal, patterns of sociability and social capital, structured around loose networks of kinship and association (Pérez-Díaz, 2002). An overview of civic engagement in Sweden suggests a similar breakdown of organized social capital, attributable to a limited role for government in the Swedish democratic model and consequential ambivalence about institutionalized forms of social capital (Rothstein, 2002). In Australia, while social capital appears to be more functional in groups with greater economic flexibility and potential gain from social change, public cynicism and public policy failure negate the impact of social capital generated (Cox, 2002). Japan is frequently cited as a country rich in social capital; however, it is experiencing similar processes of transition "from relatively closed to relatively open social capital, from reassurance-oriented to trust-generating social capital, from binding to extending social capital" (Inoguchi, 2002, p. 390).

The list of countries is exemplary and indicative of transitions that the nature of civic engagement is undergoing, as old civic habits morph into new ones that highlight the informality of civic practices, the collapse of social, cultural, political, and civic objectives, the rise of public skepticism, and the mounting pressures of work and mobility. The individual economic, socio-cultural, and political character of each country naturally informs and modifies the generation of social capital in developed societies; however, the common emphasis on values of autonomy, control, and expression requires the generation of social capital that is more flexible, so as to accommodate morphing and liquid lifestyles.

The mythos of technology is structured around the magical capabilities of innovation leading to utopia. In late modern developed democracies, temporally and geographically fluid environments realized via the capabilities of convergent technologies suggest the illusion of total control (Castoriadis, 1991; Morley, 2007). It is, in fact, a central characteristic of convergent technologies that, unlike previous communicative technologies, they do not deliver a product, service, or cultural artifact, but rather deliver the promise of ultimate control and autonomy. It should come as no surprise then that the uses of online convergent media, like the Internet, are frequently organically developed and structured around the organization, liberation, and mobilization of an individual's every-day reality. Compelled by the fluidity of this everyday reality, these technologies often afford narrative capabilities that permit the expression of identities via *despatialized simultaneity*. These enable a performative storytelling of the self, unfolding to multiple audiences and across several chronological points. Thus, the private sphere model traces the progression of a citizen who has retreated from the public sphere of interaction to a technologically enabled mobile private sphere of thought, expression, and reaction, in search of ultimate autonomy and expression.

From this perspective, civic apathy with politics can potentially be interpreted as dissatisfaction with how the state or media institutions have prioritized public and private issues, including some while excluding others. Subsequently, any deployment of online digital media is undertaken by individuals to rectify perceived inconsistencies between what the citizen deems as public, but other civic institutions have excluded from their agenda as private. Thus, individuals attempt to remedy the inconsistencies of a democratic paradox that promises plurality, yet lacks the means with which to deliver it. The private sphere also potentially reconciles the priorities of mainstream media and the greater capitalist imaginary with the personal priorities of the creative imaginary sustained by the discordant concert of conjoined private spheres. Finally, it is aligned with a contemporary understanding of the citizen, who evaluates public affairs with the self as the point of reference, and with the tools afforded him/her in post-industrial representative democracies at hand.

The citizen in a representative democracy, previously enabled within the public sphere and through civic deliberation, is now enabled via a private sphere and through the use of private media environments. This private citizen is not politically disinterested; on the contrary, this citizen is politically interested in modes that are not easily captured via aggregate measures, such as polls, and has a political appetite that is not satiated by mass-produced content. The private sphere is constructed so as to host and serve the values of autonomy, control, and self-expression central to citizens of late modern developed-country democracies. Therefore, the personalized content provided by online media fits well within this citizen's private sphere of contemplation, evaluation, and action, in which the self remains the point of reference. This citizen is alone, but not lonely or isolated. On the contrary, within the private sphere, the individual cultivates civic habits that enable him or her to connect with others on the basis of shared social, political, and cultural priorities. Five of these new habits are illustrated as emblematic of the private sphere model of civic engagement in late modern developed democracies.

Five new civic habits

1 The networked self and the culture of remote connectivity

The private sphere enables a citizen who wishes to function civically and connect with other citizens. It does so without requiring entry to public spaces that compromise the flexibility of a private and personal sphere. The private sphere is established statically through the locus of the home or the workplace, and portably through technologies of mobility, thus facilitating multi-tasking of civic and other behaviors. Therefore, the individual need not commit him/herself to the pursuit only of things civic; instead, civic obligations may be pursued alongside other social and pastime activities. For example, an individual may sign a protest petition electronically, while watching news on television, participating in background family conversation, and enjoying the comfort of their couch after a long day at work. Alternatively, a person may post a blog or a tweet that expresses personal opinion on public affairs, while on a short break from work, and in direct response to the day's current events and developments.

The private sphere does not suggest that the individual is disconnected; on the contrary, it enables connectivity from spaces that the individual delineates as private. McCarthy (2001), in *Ambient Television*, suggests that coin-operated TV spectatorship in public terminals presents a form of privacy in public, and discusses several instances of public TV viewing that presumes an out-of-home spectator that is both "captive and mobile, both receptive and hostile" (p. 100). Events broadcast on overhead screens in bars, stadiums, and public areas simultaneously connect individuals through the shared experience of viewing and interrupt immediate spheres of conversation and sociality external to the broadcast. Online convergent technologies situate the private sphere in a similar spatial context, which evokes both distance and proximity to produce narratives of social, cultural, and political relevance for the individual. The private sphere interweaves multiple configurations of public and private to suggest spaces of cultural meaning for the individual. These spaces may be located in public or private places, but what makes them private is that the individual has defined the time and space as devoted to private pursuit. These private spheres may be established in busy airport and transportation terminals, in enclosed domestic spheres, in waiting room areas, the workplace, and, in general, wherever convergent technologies of connectivity may function. They connect remotely, but may also disconnect locally. I argue that through variable affordances of online convergent technologies, especially online social networks, forms of social multi-tasking which negate local disconnection are provided.

Networked platforms of activity enabled by convergent technologies grant the private sphere civic and social legitimacy, as they effectively augment its connectivity potential. Online social networks present one such example, as they allow the individual to connect to local and remote spheres of family members, friends and acquaintances, and strong and weaker social ties. It is through association with others that civic identity and solidarity are actualized, while at the same time sustaining the control, autonomy, and self-expression capabilities of the private sphere. Social networks have always supported the formation and maintenance of existing and new social ties of variable strength, intensity, and depth. Online technologies further expand the communicative channels that individuals may dedicate to the cultivation of social networks (Wasserman & Faust, 1994; Wellman & Berkowitz, 1997). The flexibility of online digital technologies permits interaction and relations among individuals within the same networks or across networks, a variety of exchanges and ties, variable frequency of contact and intimacy, affiliation with smaller or larger, and global or local, networks formed around variable common matter (Haythornthwaite, 2000, 2001, 2002a & b, 2005; Haythornthwaite, Wellman, & Mantei, 1995; Haythornthwaite & Wellman, 1998). Frequently serving as an alternative to face-to-face interaction, online communication within or across networks has been positively associated with the generation of social capital (Hampton & Wellman, 2003; Hampton, 2002; Hampton & Wellman, 2001a & b, 2003; Wellman, Haase, Witte, & Hampton, 2001).

Social network sites extend the connectivity and mobility of the private sphere by providing online spaces that host offline and online networks of social relations. They are defined as "web-based services that allow individuals to (1) construct a public or semi-public profile within a bounded system, (2) articulate a list of other users with whom they share a connection, and (3) view and traverse their list of connections and those made by others within the system" (boyd & Ellison, 2007). Activated through the privacy of individual computer and online connections, online social networks exemplify the ability of the private sphere to sustain social contact via privately framed, technologically enabled, spaces. From this private starting point of social connectivity, presenting a profile and displaying connections with others publicly forms the basis for interaction on SNSs (boyd & Ellison, 2007; boyd & Heer, 2006; Donath, 2007; Donath & boyd, 2004). The ability of SNSs to cater to varying types of interactions, affiliations, and interests on diverse and differing platforms further magnifies the potential autonomy and control afforded by a private sphere.

What makes online social networks particularly useful for individuals entering the public realm via convergent techno-logical means is their ability to adapt to personal communication styles and routines. Allowing more controlled and managed self-presentation performances, which can be executed from the comfort of one's private surroundings, SNSs add an element of liquidity to the private sphere. Through spheres of contact accessed through SNSs, it is possible for the private sphere to evolve beyond its traditional connotations of anchored domesticity to meet the post-modern demands of mobile nomadic existences. An offline private sphere may only sustain contact among those individuals residing, even if temporarily, within its locus. Social network sites expand the number and range of individuals who may enter the privately public space of the private sphere from a variety of tempo-ral and geographic coordinates. The interaction that ensues allows the individual to retain the comfort and familiarity of the private sphere, with convenient access to tools for self-performances that are a peculiar blend of relaxed and rehearsed. Thus, the social utility of the private sphere is magnified in a three-fold way: (a) by "multiplying" the potential audiences of social contacts the individual may communicate with, including family, friends, and acquaintances; (b) by allowing the individual to sustain this social contact within a privately public and publicly private space that retains the familiarity of the private and the reach of the public; and (c) by affording presentation of the self within a mediated environment that serves the prominent values of autonomy, control, and expression for the technologically literate individual.

Multiplied social audiences are accessed through public displays of friends. Upon joining an online SNS, the individual must claim an identity, usually their actual one, which is then further confirmed and validated by establishing social connections to other registered friends. This mediated authentication of identity is based around a member profile structured as a conversational piece, and performed in concordance with the self and social ties established by the networked self online. In this context, "public displays of connection" present the center of identity performance, and are typically viewed as "a signal of the reliability of one's identity claims" (Donath & boyd, 2004, p. 73). The asynchronous temporal and spatial parameters of this self-performance potentially enhance the ability to manage impressions formed of the self, permitting the user to craft what could be considered a more controlled performance. The availability of online props affords a dramaturgical element to the performance, as individuals combine a variety of semiological references in order to produce a performance that applies to not just a single situation, but rather multiple ones and different audiences without sacrificing its coherence (Goffman, 1959).

A profile and displayed connections present a set of signals to potential audiences, which are interpreted by viewers to gauge the credibility and reliability of information that they are viewing. Donath (1998, 2007) found that individuals combine *assessment* signals, which are reliable but costly to produce or re-produce, with *conventional* signals, not as reliable, but less costly to produce, to communicate trust and identity on SNSs. Once the authenticity of identity is determined, individuals use the tools at hand to present themselves in "show, not tell" mode by pointing and connecting to individuals, groups, or cultural points of reference. For example, within the architecturally barren structure of Friendster, users display friends to suggest or "signal" aspects of their identity to potential audiences (boyd and Heer, 2006). It is also not uncommon for users to compete for who possesses the most friends, or who is connected to the most coveted friends, or friends/acquaintances with celebrity status, as a way of communicating social standing (Cassidy, 2006; Slotnik, 2007).

Ironically enough, while the needs for autonomy, control, and expression are fulfilled through the technological features of converged and asynchronous online environments, the coherence of the presentation of the self is disturbed by the collapse and multiplicity of audiences that the same convergence forces. Performing for audiences that are variably public or private, remote or close, known or unknown to the self, creates new challenges for the individual. Goffman (1959) suggested that many of our projected performances and interactions are constructed around our reading of the particular situation at hand. Thus, through a dramaturgically influenced ritual, the self traverses from the private domain of the backstage to the public domain of the front stage, where the self is presented and managed in public through an elaborate information game of concealment and disclosure. In environments that are both *privately public* and *publicly private*, the sequential arrangement of backstage and front stage is upset. The backstage no longer signals privacy and the front stage does not guarantee publicity. SNSs potentially collapse front and backstage into a single space, by allowing privately intended information to be broadcast to multiple public audiences, and delivering publicly produced information to private and intimately known audiences. Moreover, the individual must assess not one situation, but potentially an infinite number, in which the same self-performance must maintain authenticity, coherence, and relevance. Take, for instance, the cues deposited in member profiles, such as a message on Facebook "walls" or comments on shared pictures. These publicly shared comments are infused with private meaning that rarely translates across variable situations and audiences. They do not present an intentional aspect of identity performance emanating from the self. Yet, SNS users frequently interpret such cues to make inferences about the member's character (Walther, Van Der Heide, Kim, Westerman & Tom Tong, 2008). At the same time, Facebook users employ these publicly shared comments of private meaning to signal the presence of a private group, thus delineating private space in a public domain and enforcing group solidarity and cohesion (Lange, 2007; Mendelson & Papacharissi, 2008).

This complex balance of ego-centered networks that sustain private and public meanings for private and public audiences is simultaneously liberating and confining for the individual. The values of *autonomy, control,* and *expression,* prioritized in developed democracies, are generously afforded via SNSs. The technology invites expression, affords autonomy, and enables control of the self and its multiple performances. At the same time, the technology presupposes an aware and literate user who recognizes and can manage the exposure his/her self-performance will receive. Most individuals, however, share personal information openly and few modify their default privacy settings for increased protection (Gross & Acquisti, 2005). Individuals join SNSs and share information despite privacy concerns (Acquisti & Gross, 2006) while some recognize the compromising of private information but do not possess the tools or know-how to amend it (Papacharissi & Mendelson, 2010). Even though Facebook is accessible to everyone, some argue that it contains a built-in demographic bias, as not only is Internet access and literacy required to enjoy its privileges (Hargittai, 2007), but its initial user base was structured around privileged educational institutions and thus carries an American-bourgeois element (boyd, quoted in Johnson, 2007). Moreover, the economy of social network markets exploits social labor produced by the user through forms of monitoring and data mining, which effectively further commodify social and political activities online (Andrejevic, 2010). Thus, the networked nexus of the private sphere is vulnerable to the inequalities present in the public sphere. Online social networks afford flexibility and connectivity to the private sphere, but they also transfer and replicate existing elites, inequalities, and race/class/gender divides. They help attain the goals of autonomy, control, and expression, but the question then becomes, to what extent are these goals self- or democracy-serving? Autonomy, control, and expression, as realized via the social networks of the private sphere, present ego-centered needs and reflect practices structured around the self. This would suggest liberating practices for the user, but not necessarily democratizing practices for the greater society. While the social and political potential of convergent online technologies is indisputable, their democratizing affordances are questionable. It is possible that we have created technologies that have a social and political place within a democracy, but that do not inherently make democracy better. Therefore, it might make sense to frame these affordances as democratic, but not democratizing.

2 A new narcissism: blogging

Personalization, that is, the ability to organize information based on a subjective order of importance determined by the self, presents an operative feature of online media like the Internet. It is a widely accepted fact that popular applied uses of the Internet, like blogs or MySpace personal/private spaces, thrive on personalization. In *The Culture of Narcissism*, Christopher Lasch (1979) described a self-centered culture that emerged following the political turmoil of the sixties, focused on self-improvement, "wrapped in rhetoric of authenticity and awareness," and signifying "a retreat from politics and a repudiation of the recent past" (pp. 4–5). Lasch was not describing historical trends that have escaped other historians or public thinkers, who have also connected these trends more explicitly to the "privatization" of the individual, to individual and collective autonomy, and to hedonism (e.g., Castoriadis, 1986; Hesse, 1930/1968; Kondylis, 1991). Media scholars have examined how the consequences and failures of sixties alternative politics have impacted the current relationship individuals have with media or the tendency of contemporary media to abandon historical perspective (e.g., Hart, 1994; Gitlin, 1980, 1983; Patterson, 1993; Putnam, 1996; Schudson, 1998). Moreover, social and political scientists have visited the lasting impact that social, economic, cultural, and economic changes brought on by modernity have had on value and belief systems.

Terms used by these scholars have ranged from the privatization or atomization of the individual and civic action to hedonism,
to narcissism, to autonomy, to a desire for control, just to name
a few. Delving into these analytical strands would require several
volumes, yet suffice it to say that it is impossible to understand
the ramifications of blogging without situating it as a social phenomenon of an information-driven late modernity. It is within a
post-modern culture that emphasizes self-expression values that
this particular breed of civically motivated narcissism emerges.
It should be clarified at this point that the term *narcissism* is not
employed in a pejorative manner or in its pathological sense, which
would imply a personality disorder. I could easily have employed the
term *hedonism*, which carries an explicit connection to materialistic
and consumerist culture, and also describes several contemporary
civic behaviors. *Autonomy* or *desire for control* would also have
presented valid linguistic choices, but these present motives for
action; they do not describe a behavioral trend. *Narcissism* here is
employed to understand the introspection and self-absorption that
takes place in blogs and similar spaces, and to place these tendencies in historical context. Lasch's work, rather than psychological
research on narcissism as a personality disorder, serves as an apt
starting point. Narcissism is defined as a preoccupation with the
self that is self-directed, but not selfishly motivated. Narcissism is
referenced as the cultural context within which blogs are situated,
and not as a unilateral label characterizing all blogs.

Blogs are defined as web pages that consist of regular or
daily posts, arranged in reverse chronological order and archived
(Herring, Kouper, Scheidt, & Wright, 2004). Initially heralded as a
ground-breaking development in the world of reporting and media
(e.g., Sullivan, 2002), blogs bear considerable democratizing
potential as they provide media consumers with the opportunity
to become media producers (Coleman, 2005a & b). However,
despite the audience and public pulpit that blogs provide, they
typically regress to self-confessional posts that resemble diaries,
with few exceptions that engage in journalistically informed pun-
ditry (Papacharissi, 2007; Scott, 2007; Sundar, Edwards, Hu, &
Stavrositu, 2007). Research has shown that blogs can broadly be

divided into: A-list blogs (popular publicized blogs); blogs that are somewhat interconnected; and a majority of sparsely socially connected and less conversational blogs (Herring et al., 2005). At the same time, there are many instances in which bloggers exerted considerable influence over mainstream media, usually by creating noise over issues or political candidates initially marginalized by mainstream media (Kerbel & Bloom, 2005; Meraz, 2007; Tremayne, 2007; Walker Rettberg, 2008). Several major news outlets, including CNN, use blogs as "a finger on the pulse of the people" and routinely feature stories or content on what "the blogs" are reporting on a given day. Other mainstream outlets, like the *New York Times*, have incorporated blogging into their traditional reporting, and use it to provide in-depth reporting and/or indulge specific journalists' story interests. Varied and diverse as they may be, news blogs frequently function as gateways for mainstream media coverage.

Blogs, video blogs (vlogs), and similar expressions may be symptomatic of a hedonistic and materialistic culture, which, in an Althusserian sense, "interpellates" its citizens as consumers. Political thoughts expressed on blogs are narcissistically motivated in that they are not created with the explicit purpose of contributing to a public sphere, the commons, or heightening civic engagement. While it is true that occasionally they impact mainstream media and public opinion in a significant manner, blog content is determined by subjective inclinations and tendencies based on a personal evaluation of content. Quantitative analysis of blogs finds them to be largely self-referential (Papacharissi, 2007) and motivated by personal fulfillment (Kaye, 2007). Even news-oriented, A-list blogs present a *mélange* of public and private information that is subjectively arrived at and removed from Western standards of the journalistic profession (objective or partisan). Bloggers blog simply because they want to.

This particular breed of political expression is self-serving and occasionally self-directed, but should not be mischaracterized as selfish. Similarly, Lasch understood narcissistic behavior as structured around the self, but not motivated by selfish desire. Ironically, narcissistic behavior is motivated by the desire to connect the self to society. Lasch acknowledged the insecurity embedded in narcissism, but proceeded to place that narcissism within the "sense of endless possibility" pitted against "the banality of the social order" that contemporary Americans find themselves overcome by (1979, p. 11). According to Lasch, the self-preoccupation associated with the culture of narcissism "arises not from complacency but from desperation" in a society that does not provide a clear distinction between public and private life (p. 26). In moments of variable insight, bloggers engage in typical secondary strategies of the narcissist: "pseudo self-insight, calculating seductiveness, nervous, self-deprecatory humor" (Lasch, 1979, p. 33). The new Narcissus, according to Lasch, gazes at his/her own reflection "not so much in admiration as in unremitting search of flaws, signs of fatigue, decay," structuring a performance of the self that is reminiscent of the theatrical. In blogs, the expression of public opinion on private forums (or the expression of private opinion on a public forum – the blogger constantly plays with this distinction) becomes a carefully orchestrated performance with the Other in mind.

Alternatively, late modern narcissism is resurrected and reconnected to ascetic practices of self-reflection and self-expression by Sennett (1974), who argues against the common-sense view that self-absorption and asceticism are contrary. It is this widely regarded misconception, grounded in religiously infused understandings of asceticism, however, that situates narcissistic self-absorption as the opposite of ascetically motivated introspection. Yet, Sennett (1974) suggests, asceticism and narcissism have much in common, including obsession with personal feelings, validation of these feelings, and a projection of the self into the world. He suggests that in modern societies, the ascetic character of narcissism is cultivated as a way to justify the self through introspective withdrawal, then reconnects the self socially through narcissistic practices. Narcissism involves analysis and introspection: a great deal of examination of one's own reflection. The Narcissus, in Hesse's conceptualization, focuses on both the negative and the positive aspects of their reflection; this introspection can be a valuable tool for self-actualization.

A healthy dose of narcissism for citizens connects well with democracy. It allows citizens to self-reflect, to analyze, and, via blogging, to "get a lot of things off their chest." Self-reflection promotes self-understanding, and, as Castoriadis (2007) argues, "self-understanding is a necessary condition for autonomy. One cannot have an autonomous society that would fail to turn back upon itself, that would not interrogate itself about its motives, its reasons for acting, its deep-seated [*profondes*] tendencies . . . The self-reflective activity of an autonomous society depends essentially upon the self-reflective activity of the humans who form that society" (p. 151). This does not apply to everyone, as when journalists exhibit narcissistic trends, the result is self-serving journalism. For citizen bloggers, however, a healthy dose of narcissism enables intense self-reflection, followed by liberated self-expression. Narcissism, in Sennett's (1974) terms, "takes the idea of the involuntary disclosure of character to its logical extreme" (p. 336). Blogs present the contemporary terrain where ascetic practices of narcissism untangle the complex relation of the self to its own self, and, by extension, to the democratic environments that it inhabits.

The subjective focus of blogs and similar forums encourages plurality of voices and expands the public agenda. While narcissistically motivated, blogs are democratizing in a unique manner. As Bimber (2000) argues, while online technologies "contribute toward greater fragmentation and pluralism in the structure of civic engagement," their tendency "to deinstitutionalize politics, fragment communication, and accelerate the pace of the public agenda and decision-making may undermine the coherence of the public sphere" (pp. 332–3). With their focus on making a private agenda public, blogs challenge the established public agenda in an anarchic manner. This lack of coordination or concentrated civic objectives limits the contribution to the public sphere, and exemplifies how online technologies enhance democracy in ways tangential to, but not directly connected with, that sphere. While blogs and similar vehicles (e.g., YouTube) dilute the agenda-setting function of traditional news sources, they still present personalized media environments (Swanson, 2000), and, as such, make limited contribution to the greater-good objectives of the public sphere.

The unique contribution of blogs lies not in enabling the public good, but rather in challenging the premises upon which it rests. Their function is expressive first, and deliberative only by accident. Sennett (1974) suggests that a society mobilizing narcissism "gives rein to a principle of expression," which makes "artifice and convention seem suspect" (p. 336). Thus, blogs and similar media are best understood in terms of their potential for debasing the stability of political environments, including democracies and non-democracies, rather than revitalizing the structures within which they come to be. As opinion leaders, bloggers use their own blogs as public pulpits to express opinions on public affairs (e.g., Scott, 2007; Tremayne, 2007). Through a web of interconnections with other citizen journalists, activists, and commentators, and with conventional media, they may be able, on occasion, to create sufficient noise to allow a direct impact on the media, public, and policy agendas (Walker Rettberg, 2008). As watchdogs, they employ technology to draw attention to issues marginalized or ignored by mainstream media (e.g., Meraz, 2007; Sundar, Edwards, Hu, & Stourositu 2007). Robinson (2009) further suggests that blogging allows citizen journalists to find their own place in their story, by interpolating narratives of the self with mainstream narratives. Blogs acquire meaning as they successfully dilute the agenda-setting influence of traditional news sources, to present novel, subjective interpretation of what presents news.

Therefore, such atomized uses of online media by individuals in their homes do not constitute a public or a public sphere (Dahlgren, 2005), but they do successfully make the political environment more "porous" (Blumler & Gurevitch, 2000). Blogging should not be mistaken for journalism, nor should it be mistaken for a public sphere. Its value lies in demonstrating the conflict between what is private and public, a venerable and timeless conflict that is stressed by online technologies. The type of self-absorption we see in blogs is a play, a constant game with what others define as public or private and what the blogger believes should be defined as public or private. Blogger priorities here lie in broadening and overlapping private and public agendas, not reviving the public sphere.

3 The rebirth of satire and subversion: YouTube

Recent research on how citizens make use of online media world-wide indicates that, while political use of new media is vast, it does not fit the mold of the Habermasian public sphere and promotes direct democracy selectively. Citizens are drawn primarily to interest group and non-partisan websites (Cornfield, Rainie, & Horrigan, 2003), but still prefer websites of major media outlets or TV for information on public affairs over Internet-based news organizations (Kohut, 2003). Availability of information alone is unable to sustain and encourage civic engagement (Marcella, Baxter, & Moore, 2002). Citizens online veer away from the conventions of news releases and endorsements to the informality of online polls and political jokes and cartoons (Cornfield, Rainie, & Horrigan, 2003).

Politicians employ digital media mostly to conduct political research, enhance two-step-flow communication with other media and opinion leaders, invite donations to political causes, and publicize news releases and endorsement (Cornfield, 2004). Political party websites are successful in reaching out to young voters, but are unable to connect with people who have so far remained aloof towards politics (J. L. Jensen, 2003; Boogers & Voerman, 2003). Online political discussions that feature politicians do enjoy greater participation, but are frequently dominated by politicians who employ them to advocate for their agendas (J. L. Jensen, 2003). By contrast, the behavior of citizens seeking political information online reflects a preference for the playful, non-mainstream, and unexpected.

Nowhere is this more prevalent than in the remixed content vaults of YouTube, which has been described as "Easy to use and does not tell you what to do" (Boutin, 2006). Others highlight the diversity of content featured, making mention of the "Many Tribes of YouTube" (Heffernan, 2007), or the authenticity of communication featured (Story, 2007; Young, 2007). YouTube contains vast amounts of audiovisual content, presented in an unstructured format that makes the site virtually impossible to monitor or regulate. Some of this content violates copyright, in that it manifestly reproduces content already copyrighted by other entities. Other types of content present creative re-workings of media content in ways that endorse the audience member as media producer, and promote political satire and dialogue. The main draw is that YouTube user-generated content serves a variety of purposes, ranging from catching a politician in a lie to impromptu karaoke, with no restrictions. Thriving upon a culture that emphasizes sound bites, and, more recently, image bites, YouTube has become a powerful tool and challenge for political campaigning (Castells, 2009; Grabe & Bucy, 2009). Its pluralistic politics afford all the opportunity to publicly embarrass and be embarrassed. More importantly, the site facilitates expression, reassures citizens of their autonomy, and offers individuals some form of control of the public agenda.

Where blogging provides the pulpit, YouTube provides the irreverence, humor, and unpredictability necessary for rejuvenating political conversation trapped in conventional formulas. As participatory citizen journalism, YouTube illustrates a contemporary take on the editorial cartoon and satire, elements of reporting that typically generate more emotional reactions, yet are practically extinct from news portals at present. It is no accident that YouTube generated early attention by routinely featuring satirical quips from *The Daily Show with Jon Stewart*. The prominence of satirical content reveals a playful mood that results in a creative and nonsensical pastiche of content, that is befitting of post-modern political tastes and orientations. YouTube content completes the media and news sphere that the monitorial citizen scans while surveying the political environment, by adding various and diverse takes on political reality. YouTube also provides an opportunity for expression different from conventional mobilization, expression of opinion, or protest. Not all issues on our radars warrant these types of reaction; some simply evoke sarcasm, humor, or satire, which are equally important forms of political thought and expression.

Blogging and YouTube frequently work collaboratively, as would be expected of convergent media, cross-referencing content. The collective and combined video-blogosphere further enables subversion and feeds the need for satire and self-criticism in contemporary democracies. Blogs do not present or replace journalism, and any such consideration would undermine their potential. The independent citizen operates as the accidental journalist, engaging in information-gathering that is determined by whim, personal preference, and indulgence in personal interests. Within a typical representative democracy, the monitorial citizen surveys information but has limited avenues for becoming involved, should it become necessary to do so. However, within the more pluralized political environment convergent technologies enable, monitorial citizens are afforded: (a) a wider scope of issue and coverage to monitor, (b) guidance on issues based on standards that resemble their own, and (c) a direct route for mobilization and exerting influence. For citizens of developed and contemporary democracies, net-based technologies provide the tools with which to challenge what is defined as private and what is defined as public, and thus a way to challenge public agendas.

4 Social media news aggregation and the plurality of collaborative filtering

The potential to influence and modify the hierarchy of the news and policy agendas extends beyond the blogosphere and YouTube, to the online public spaces frequented by everyday news readers. User-generated content presented via citizen media or blogs may pluralize the news agenda, but it involves content creation. Socially oriented and peer-supported platforms enable practices like social book-marking, file storage, and content sharing, and pluralize the news agenda via the practice of content consumption. Personalization and customization of web content by the user is not a new trend, and has always presented an alluring, yet not an inherently democratizing, aspect of web use. It does, however, allow users to select and promote a personalized news feed. Peer-to-peer news sharing engines, in particular, such as Digg, Reddit, Netscape, or Newsvine, allow users to determine and vote on the news they deem important, thus possibly upsetting the hierarchy of news making and pluralizing the news agenda. Citizens thus inject their perspective into the news spectrum through the practice of readership and promotion of news items they deem important. By endorsing stories salient to the individual, audiences send direct messages to news producers about the types of news stories that matter to their everyday lives. Thus, the habit of reading the news, once a passive and informative pursuit, empowers the citizen who chooses to endorse it or not. The selection and endorsement of news content could potentially render news generation and cultures more participatory, but it also requires readers to transform into "citizen marketers" of content discovered and shared on these sites (McConnell & Huba, 2006).

There are a variety of theoretical perspectives through which media theorists may explicate this phenomenon to appreciate its impact on networked democratic societies. First, the practice of submitting, reading, and endorsing a particular news story affirms, contradicts, or expands the mainstream news agenda and engages readers as news gatekeepers. Empowered with agenda-setting privileges, non-content-creating audiences find a way to trade in their individual content preferences for gatekeeping currency. Second, their inclusion in gatekeeping elites allows citizen gatekeepers to endorse, reject, or modify news agendas, and potentially related policy and public agendas. Since prominent presence in a news agenda grants issues credibility and visibility, social media news aggregators allow citizens direct access to an agenda they could previously only be passive observers of. Third, the ability to exert gatekeeping influence positions audience members as the third stage in what appears to be a three-step flow, thus extending Lazarsfeld, Gaudet and Berelson's (1944) two-step flow of news and opinion from news organizations to prominent opinion leaders, and then to the public (K. B. Jensen, 2009). In a three-step-flow model, the public possesses opinion-leading privileges which allow it to function, en masse, as consumer and modifier of news content. News information then flows from news organizations to opinion leaders and networked publics simultaneously, and not sequentially, to finally reach a larger audience that consists of news organizations, opinion leaders and audience publics grouped together.

The democratizing potential of social news aggregators is

defined by their ability to afford power. Audience members do not possess equal access to technology, literacy, or the will to place themselves in the news-producing and public opinion formation equation. For those who are digitally equipped, knowledgeable, and interested, there is no guarantee that news preferences will deviate from the mainstream and contribute perspectives that are different. Finally, invigorating as the ability to support, abort, or influence news content may be, the avenues for involving audiences are riddled with binary choices that echo marketing practices and are far removed from deliberative democratic models. Granting a news item a virtual "thumbs-up-or-down" confines audiences to unrealistic, predetermined, and polarized positions that have plagued public opinion polling for decades and have been connected to viewer cynicism about the political process (Cappella & Jamieson, 1997; Herbst, 1993). Moreover, social networks and news stories sharing networks overlap allowing smaller communities of friends or bloggers collaborative filtering power that impacts the distributions of news stories. Thus, a popular few may dominate the news aggregator agendas, heightening an echo-chamber effect that leads to several people repeating and reproducing the opinions of a few (Cappella & Jamieson, 2008; Meraz, 2009).

Preliminary research findings support several of these trends. In a recent study, Meraz (2009) compared the power law distribution of news content on social media news aggregator sites Digg, Reddit, Newsvine, and Netscape, to find variable power curves, corresponding to different audience needs and preferences. Most news content featured on these sites was political, although entertainment news was prominent and diluted the civic potential of the medium. The "stickiness" of news stories was moderate, indicating a disposability of content that might further mitigate the long-term impact of participatory news making. Interestingly enough, Digg news content was characterized by a gentler power law curve and was less biased in favor of elites. Both Digg and Reddit linked to a greater variety of news sources, approximately half of which tended to be citizen media. Newsvine and Netscape were more prone to elite bias and obtained their stories from traditional media sources and elites. All sites served as potential gatekeepers or gatewatchers for particular communities of users, with Digg leaning heavily towards more technology-oriented stories and users, while the remaining three catered to political news and could thus be potentially supportive of civic engagement. These findings indicate that online technologies can be most meaningful in filtering undercover news items into the news mainstream, as is the case with Digg and its niche angle on technology news.

The tendency for online technologies to work optimally when put to use to cover stories that have not been picked by mainstream news outlets is further evidenced by prominent content on blogs, YouTube, and online activism sites. In the context of collaborative filtering sites like Digg, this is further documented by the voting logic of contributing members, which tends to favor that which is not present in other media, whatever that may be, for a particular context. In an analysis of content that Digg users "digg," Halavais (2009) found that comments or stories containing humor, satire, and profanity received the most diggs, which could have been positive or negative. Halavais (2009) suggested the diggers deviate from the rationalized Habermasian model of deliberation, veering closer to amorphous and hierarchical modes of conversation that are motivated more by upsetting the order of news than by affirming it. Indeed, much like other interactions that formulate online, these conversations are spontaneous and form organically and in response to the referent community of users. The users' preference for humor, satire, and the unpredictability of profanity affirms the need for political conversation that adheres to norms other than those instilled by mainstream media and civic institutions, and further solidifies the cultivation of a vernacular founded upon the need to simply speak *otherwise* about public affairs.

It should be noted that the above present gradual trends, as the majority of the population still makes use of conventional news sources. A recent Pew Research Center for the People and the Press report revealed that 46 percent of American adults are so-called *traditionalists*: an older, less educated and less affluent news audience segment that mostly gets its news from TV and finds visually based stories easier to understand (Kohut, 2008). However, a growing proportion of news readers (36 percent) are either *integrators* or *net newsers*, meaning that they get their news from both traditional sources and the Internet, or mostly from the Internet (Kohut, 2008). Related data sets reveal that net newsers and integrators reflect cohorts that are moving away from "appoint-ment media," that is, watching TV newscasts at the appointed hour or reading the newspaper in the morning (Rainie, 2008). These users are more likely to check news throughout the day, acciden-tally discover news stories while looking for other things online from home or work, and treat news as a participatory process (Rainie, 2008). The participatory news gathering affordances of news media may fragmentize news publics into issue-specific cohorts, but also allow these cohorts to self-organize and contrib-ute, without being required to know every aspect of news-based reality (Ito, 2003). In this participatory news environment, the job of the journalist becomes more conversational, as journalism can work towards connecting the decentralized nexus of citizen-fueled media (Gillmor, 2009) or to "force the intersection of the net-work's centers and margins, and to introduce information to the network that it would otherwise ignore" (Rutigliano, 2009).

The democratizing potential of citizen media can then be located in the synergistic power of journalism, and the dynam-ics of organically driven deliberation, as these form to respond to events developing in democratic and non-democratic countries. During the contested June 2009 Iran elections, news audiences turned to independent Iranian citizen tweeters who reported their own stories, as foreign media were confined to their hotel rooms by the government, and cell phones, text messages, and access to SNSs or search engines were jammed or tracked (Huffington Post, June 17, 2009). Tweeters blasted conventional news media sources like CNN for not doing enough to cover the story. The momentum gained by independent citizen coverage of the election led the US government to intervene, not in Iranian internal affairs, but, rather, in Twitter server maintenance schedules, and request that Twitter delay a network upgrade so as to protect the interests of Iranians tweeting live events (Grossman, 2009). Concurrently, several websites, including BoingBoing.net magazine, published cyberwar guides for participating constructively in the Iranian election protests without compromising the personal information and safety of independent Iranian tweeters (Doctorow, 2009). Journalists could then piece together these decentralized and atomized reports to tell a cohesive and complete story, using traditional and newer media. In this sense, democratizing potential rests not solely with net-based citizen media, but rather with the collaborative environments created. Net-based technologies interact with remediated forms of reporting the news, and thus allow us to record, reflect on, and react to our collective existence. These newer civic practices are net-based *and* networked, meaning that they work optimally as their individual potentialities are combined to form an uninterrupted string of engagement that feeds off its different components and produces a compounded effect that is ultimately democratizing. This nexus of collaborative social networks – blogs, tweets, video-blogs, YouTube videos, diggs, and other forms of citizen media – amalgamates around the self and the territory of the self – that is, the private sphere, which serves as the starting point and the core of all such activity.

5 The agonistic pluralism of online activism

More than 10 years ago, protesters gathered in Seattle to protest against the economic and cultural globalization, in one of the most sizable and audible civil protests of the past few decades. What was striking about this protest, besides its size, was its ability to coordinate a variety of activist groups with varying goals to express the single collective objective of anti-globalization. This coordination of a variety of networked anti-globalization efforts was effected through online communication, in what appears to be one of the most memorable examples of an online-spawned show of solidarity. Social movements have become transnational in reach and transitioned to a networked organization. Diani (2000) suggests that, beyond going global, these movements are becoming virtual, thus providing new ways for citizens to engage with domestic and international causes. While e-mail remains a focal modality of communication and collaboration, most social movements actively employ the Internet to enroll, deliberate with, and mobilize their constituents.

Vegh (2003) organizes the subversive efforts of online activism into the following three categories: awareness/advocacy, organization/mobilization and action/reaction. Expressions of online activism typically evolve through these three phases, by employing Internet-based platforms to enable engagement with the social problem at hand and mobilize constituents. Online technologies permit the spontaneous and organic gathering of protest groups or flash mobs, in ways that are more interconnected, intelligent, and potentially powerful or "smart" (Rheingold, 2002). In the USA, MoveOn.org presents what resembles an online shopping arcade of political causes and petitions, typically structured around mainstream political candidates and issues, while Meet-up groups provide avenues for online and offline action and reaction strategies (Chadwick, 2007). Globally, platforms like Facebook allow remotely located individuals to connect over shared interests and beliefs, and donate to, and recruit support for, the causes they are interested in. Finally, hacktivism promotes a different form of activism and protest, effected through the direct subversion and manipulation of technological infrastructure to construct a political message. Frequently aligned with domestic or global activism agendas, denial-of-service attacks, forms of online vandalism, uploading of viruses and mass mailings all present forms of what Jordan (2008) terms *hacking the social*.

Several critics point out that the specialization and customization of activism tailored to personal tastes could lead to a tribalization of the global issues agenda, or a cyberbalkanization of political discourse (Sunstein, 2001). Furthermore, encouraging as online atomized demonstrations of activist unity may be, they frequently are emblematic of a *disunified multitude*: a collection of individuals coming together for shared causes, but otherwise not possessing the cohesive solidarity of the people. Contemporary expressions of online activism reflect the continued distancing from a shared understanding of the common good and an emphasis on issue-based politics and publics, first described by Dahl (1961), and revisited by several, including Melucci (1996), who explicitly connected them to identity politics, the self, and the new heterogeneous character of social movements. These self-driven iterations of collective identities have been associated with the cultural context of a more "reflexive", or "liquid" society (e.g., Bauman, 2005; Beck, Giddens, & Lash, 1994; Giddens, 1990).

Research supports the ability of digital media to connect and sustain subversive movements of a liquid and fleetingly collective nature. Subversion of mainstream political objectives by alternative movements, while not built in to the traditional Habermasian model, presents an operative aptitude of digital media. The role of the Internet in shaping the anti-globalization movement specifically highlights this aptitude, and fits better within Fraser's model of counter-publics that compete to articulate a voice within the public sphere. The Zapatistas' use of the Internet for political subversion presents a renowned example of innovative mobilization (e.g., Langman, 2005). In various anti-globalization protests mounted across nations, anti-globalization web platforms were instrumental to: (a) establishing movement formation, (b) shaping movement collective identity, and (c) mobilizing movement participants and organizations in a fluid manner (Van Aelst & Walgrave, 2002). The Internet was central to Seattle's Indymedia activist efforts (Pickard, 2006), but also to consensus building and mobilization of Code Pink, a self-identified women's movement for peace (Simone, 2006). Online technologies tend to reinforce existing patterns of political participation, which primarily serve traditional activists and/or citizens more active than the norm (Davis, 1999; Norris, 1999). Similarly, the Internet is essential to non-profit and community associations seeking access to the mainstream media agenda (Jensen, Danziger, & Venkatesh, 2007; Kenix, 2007). There is general support of the hypothesis that online media are effective in mobilizing political expression and serving as complements or alternatives to traditional media (Shah, Cho, Eveland, & Kwak, 2005).

In societies that are undergoing political transition, access to alternative media online becomes important in different ways. For instance, for users in Russia and the Ukraine, sites of online-only newspapers are of primary importance, and online versions of offline news outlets, along with politicians' websites, only minimally used (Semetko & Krasnoboka, 2003). Similarly, in a study of advocacy blogs in Kyrgystan, a former Soviet republic of Central Asia, Kulikova and Perlmutter (2007) found that *samizdat* (unofficial) blogs provided information not available through mainstream media, but essential in articulating vocal opposition to the republic's leadership and supporting the "tulip revolution." In phenomenally politically stable societies, hacktivism groups like Netstrike, Electrohippies, and the Electronic Disturbance Theater create acts of civil disobedience through manipulation of technological infrastructure, thus upsetting technological and civic continuity (Jordan, 2008).

It is apparent that politically interested, activism-prone citizens go online to complement or substitute their uses of traditional communication and directly represent their opinions. This specific mode of civic engagement and activism is more fluid, in that it engages with public affairs and public opinion at will, at variable times, with variable duration and commitment. Aligned with Schudson's (1998) monitorial approach to civic duty, as well as Howard's (2006) thin, shadow, and private citizen modalities, these fleeting forms of engagement with activist causes possess an atomized motivation and collective aspirations. Pluralistically formed, activist platforms like MoveOn.org or Facebook present a menu of activist causes, suggesting variable levels of intensity of involvement to match citizen preferences. This customization of activism is congruent with the personalizable *modus operandi* of convergent online technologies, but it has little in common with cultural activism movements of the sixties which may have been characterized by a fragmentation, but never an atomized structure. Certainly, this activist mentality may be inspired by political ideals that fueled class-based revolts of the seventeenth, eighteenth, and nineteenth centuries, but it is sustained by the private efforts of individuals who scale causes to fit their own needs, rather than adjusting their needs for the greater cause. This particular brand of activism and political engagement is carving the civic vernacular of younger cohorts who integrate digital cultures seamlessly into their everyday routines of Internet surfing and online socializing (Montgomery, 2009; Montgomery & Gottlieb-Robbles, 2006).

These atomized expressions of social activism of variable

intensity, life-expectancy, and effect reflect a move to newer modes of civic engagement, which might be understood better through Mouffe's (2005) proposal of agonistic pluralism and agonistic confrontation. Agonistic pluralism is formulated in contrast to the dialogic pluralism of the public sphere, and is aimed at radically transforming existing power relations. Mouffe (2005) employed the concept in a different context, to specifically call for the reinsertion of right and left into everyday politics. Still, the concept is useful in understanding the effect of online subversive movements on democracy. While not all instances of subversion described here have successfully destabilized the existing power structure, they originated as adversarial, possessing elements of what Mouffe (2005) terms a *conflictual consensus*, and attempt a real confrontation based on a shared set of rules, and despite disparate individual positions (p. 52). Mouffe defined agonism as a "we/they relation" where the conflicting parties, although acknowledging that they are adversaries, operate on common symbolic ground and see themselves as belonging to the same association. In this context, "the task of democracy is to transform antagonism into agonism" (p. 20). While agonists do not function outside the spectrum of the public sphere, they are less concerned with public accord, and more with self-expression and voicing disagreement. Thus, the direct representation and subversive capabilities of online media enable agonistic expressions of dissent that do not necessarily empower the public sphere, but enhance democracy by decentralizing its core and opening it up to disagreement, rather than agreement.

The private sphere and the networked citizen

The newer civic habits cultivated within a private sphere express the plasticity of public and private boundaries through the production and use of mediated spaces that advocate a private sociality, and a networked, but not traditionally engaged, practice of citizenship. Understanding the private sphere involves rethinking the spatiality of the praxis of citizenship, as it develops on planes of social, cultural, political, and economic activities that are converged, and is

shaped around an agenda that is personal. The production of mediated spaces is central to this private citizenship modality, which
affords promises of autonomy but does not guarantee privacy.
More importantly, the ability to balance technologically enabled
mobility with the fixity of the personally imposed boundaries of the
private sphere carves a citizen model that is adaptable and flexible.
But is it civic?

The private sphere is empowering, liquid, and reflexive. But what
happens to the public sphere when all political action retreats to the
private sphere? This transition from the prominent public realm to
private spaces could equal alienation, and a loss of Arendt's (1970)
"in-between" bond. It is precisely this "in-between" connection,
formed between the individual and fellow humans, that, as individuals act civically from the networked locus of the private sphere,
is filled in by online digital media. Online technologies possess
reflexive architectures, responsive to the needs of multiple private
spheres, which provide connectivity and negate isolation.

Much of the process of civic engagement involves the uneasy
transition from the personal to the political. In the past, transitioning from the personal to the political implied a corresponding
passage from private interest to public affairs. This permitted a
neater categorization of public and private activities, and a clearer
delineation of the social from the cultural, the economic, and
the political. However, the cultural logic of capitalist production,
together with the properties of electronic media, augmented by
networked and converged technologies, rearrange the personal-to-
political, and private-to-public, continuums. Activities may possess
public and private essence, imperatives may be personal and political, communication may be intimate and mediated, and audiences
may be individual or multiplied. I argue that in the private sphere
neither the personal nor the political are prevalent, but rather a
peculiar mixture of both, which simultaneously renders citizenship
less political than it was in the past, but also more autonomously
defined. This implies that the shift from the personal to the political, part of the political socialization of citizens, never takes place
or is no longer relevant. It is difficult for the networked citizen
to escape the personalization of politics, as the private sphere is

mediated and media-based, and thus dominated by self-interest. To the extent that mediated narratives dominating the private sphere include discourse on collective struggle, it is possible to observe a transition from the personal to the political, similar to that characteristic of citizenship modalities of the past. However, the more personally focused and individually customized the discourses are that enter the private sphere, the more personalized the resulting civic action and citizen will be.

But the citizen entering the networked cocoon of the private sphere is not interested in the civic obligations of the past, and associates citizenship primarily with autonomy, control, and the ability to question authority, and secondarily with the ability to do so collectively. The allure of the private sphere as a civic mobile cocoon lies in its ability to provide the illusion of civic direct control, for publics and individuals hailed in contemporary democracies via the restrictive logic of representation. Sustaining a fantasy of total control, the private sphere is comforting for individuals who experience privacy as a luxury good, intimacy in mediated form, and place and time decoupled.

The concept of a connected, yet private, sphere, which is empowered by interlaced and overlapping spheres of public and private activities that map its geography, may be explained more effectively through a visual representation. *Parliament of reality*, a permanent installation on the Bard College campus produced by the artist Olafur Eliasson, was introduced earlier in this volume as a way of connecting the public/private binary to the practice of democracy. This contemporary take on a parliament is located on a constructed island and connects to the campus via a tunnel bridge. The privacy of the deliberative island is juxtaposed against the public realm of the campus; the two are connected, yet distinct spaces, that lend themselves to different behaviors. What is even more interesting and relevant to the idea of the private sphere, however, is the stainless steel latticework tunnel employed to access the island. The tunnel bridge is composed of a series of elliptical circles or hollow spheres, which are based on the pattern of the island's floor and gradually morph into different ellipses as the tunnel bridge and the public sphere island meet. As visitors cross the bridge, the

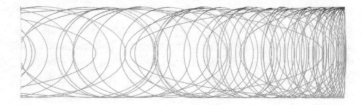

Figure 6: *Visualization of* Parliament of reality, *detail, 2009*
© *2009 Olafur Eliasson*

tunnel's escalation of interlocking elliptical circles appears to shift, gradually altering space and the way in which visitors temporally perceive themselves connecting to space. A conceptual diagram of this tunnel is presented in image 6, as an illustrative evocation of the architectural and spatial foundation of the private sphere.

I propose this as the metaphor by which we situate the private sphere in everyday life and the way in which we understand (and not prescribe) the place of online technology within a democracy. As such, the private sphere is a sphere of connection and not isolation, as it serves primarily to connect the personal to the political, and the self to the polity and society. Functioning primarily as a technologically equipped bridge of overlapping and networked spheres, this sphere simulates the enclosure of a tunnel, or a closed-in circular structure that creates space, shape-shifts, and reformulates primarily to serve the function of connection. In doing so – that is, in connecting – it also gradually alters and is altered by the self's perception of space (see image 7). And in shape-shifting, it also illuminates the function of online technologies in a democracy: to connect, to create new space, and to elude obligatory democratization.

The emphasis on connection, rather than struggle, carries important consequences for our understanding of how individual private spheres define, and exert power over, one another. Acknowledging that power is not a constant, but, rather, a potential, accessed in a variety of ways, acceptance of a private sphere model would suggest a privatized model of power. This would

Figure 7: Parliament of reality, *2006–2009. Concrete, stone, stainless steel, water, trees, other plants. Dimensions variable, CCS Bard and The Luma Foundation. Photo: Jaime Henderson.* © 2009 *Olafur Eliasson*

imply that power in the private sphere, as opposed to power in the public sphere, may not be as explicitly connected to class struggle as some Marxist theory (e.g., Gramsci, 1971; Poulantzas, 1978) would presume, although it certainly remains subject to the economics of capitalist organization. Concurrently, while the expressive affordances of the private sphere might suggest a form of power that is discursively alluded to, stated, or exercised, the discursive strategies deployed to communicate this power reflexively adjust to fit the priorities of the personal and the political (e.g., Foucault, 1980). Agonistic and discursive at the same time, the narrative of power that is constructed within the private sphere requires a reconciliation of the variety of theoretical approaches that deal with power, including Foucauldian discursive approaches and structural analyses of power. Castells (2009) effects such a reconciliation by defining power as "the relational capacity that enables a social actor to influence asymmetrically the decisions of other social actor(s) in ways that favor the empowered actor's will, interests, and values" (p. 10). This definition permits an appreciation for the reflexive properties of the private sphere while also acknowledging the structural impediments to its reach, as well as the potential for privately motivated actors to claim power via individually produced narratives.

The private sphere is the result of the combined effect of a multiplicity of economic, cultural, social, and political contexts, which were presented in detail in the preceding chapters. The realities and conflicts of public and private interests, as they converge over socio-cultural, political, and economic landscape, are well embedded within its latticework structure – a structure that shifts and reforms in response to the discursive practices of the individual, much like Eliasson's structure. The power that is afforded by the technological architectures of the private sphere emerges in networked mode, thus establishing the autonomy of each private sphere, as well as the collective power of conjoined private spheres. And, because the affordances of online technologies, are, above all, connective, the potential for power lies in the ability of autonomous spheres to connect. Thus, we notice the most impressive illustrations of collectively practiced digital democracy around occasions where technology fostered connection. Relatively powerless in conventional representative democratic environments, networked citizens claim their power through autonomously exerted acts of expression and connection. And, thus, the elevated mobile devices, raised in salute to the newly elected US President, signify solidarity, but also emphasize singularity, in contrast to flags, flag pins, and other symbolic artifacts of the past, which emphasized unequivocal unity.

This book is not about power; it is about connections that occur within the frame of a digitally practiced democracy. But democracy is about the distribution of power, and as this newer civic vernacular morphs into a canon for practicing citizenship, it would behoove us to understand, conceptually, as well as empirically, the distribution of power that technologies afford. The meaning of the political lies in the ability to express dissent, to think differently.

To the extent that the private sphere affords the autonomy, control, and expressive capabilities that enable dissent, it effectively reconciles the personal with the political in a way that enables connection with like-minded individuals. The private sphere, as metaphor, describes and explains the mechanisms for civic connections in contemporary democracies. Its value is descriptive and explanatory, but not prescriptive. Far from a recipe for democracy, the private sphere is an attempt at new space and a new sociality.

References

Abramson, J. B., Arterton, F. C. & Orren, G. R. (1988). *The Electronic Commonwealth: The Impact of New Media Technologies on Democratic Politics*. New York: Basic Books.

Acquisti, A. & Gross, R. (2006). Imagined communities: Awareness, information sharing, and privacy on the Facebook. In P. Golle & G. Danezis (eds.), *Proceedings of the 6th Workshop on Privacy Enhancing Technologies* (pp. 36–58). Cambridge: Robinson College.

Agre, P. E. (2002). Real-time politics: the Internet and the political process. *Information Society*, 18(5), 311–31.

Akdeniz, Y. (2002). Anonymity, democracy, and cyberspace. *Social Research*, 69(1), 223–37.

Althaus, S. L. & Tewksbury, D. (2000). Patterns of Internet and traditional media use in a networked community. *Political Communication*, 17, 21–45.

Althusser, L. (1970/1998). Ideology and ideological state apparatuses. In J. Rivkin & M. Ryan (eds.), *Literary Theory: An Anthology* (pp. 294–304). Malden, MA: Blackwell Publishers.

Anderson, B. (1983). *Imagined Communities*. London: Verso.

Anderson, J. Q. & Rainie, L. (2006). The Future of the Internet II. *Pew Internet & American Life Project*, www.pewinternet.org (accessed June 2009).

Andrejevic, M. (2003). *Reality TV: The Work of Being Watched*. New York: Rowman & Littlefield Publishers.

(2004). The web cam subculture and the digital enclosure. In N. Couldry & A. McCarthy (eds.), *MediaSpace: Place, Scale and Culture in a Media Age* (pp. 193–209). London: Routledge.

(2010). Social network exploitation. In Z. Papacharissi (ed.), *The Networked Self: Identity, Community and Culture on Social Network Sites*. New York: Routledge.

Ang, I. (1996). *Living Room Wars*. London: Routledge.

Appadurai, A. (1996). *Modernity at Large: Cultural Dimensions of Globalization.* Minneapolis: University of Minnesota Press.

Arendt, H. (1958). *The Human Condition.* Chicago: University of Chicago Press.

— (1970). *Man in Dark Times.* New York: Harcourt Brace.

Ariés, P. (1962). *Centuries of Childhood: A Social History of Family Life.* New York: Vintage.

Ariés, P., Veyne, P., Duby, G. & Goldhammer, A. (1987–91). *A History of Private Life.* 5 vols. Cambridge, MA: Harvard University Press.

— (1993). *A History of Private Life: Revelations of the Medieval World.* Cambridge, MA: Harvard University Press.

Aristotle (2004). *Politics.* Trans. B. Jowett. Sioux Falls, SD: NuVision.

Arterton, F. C. (1987). *Teledemocracy: Can Technology Protect Democracy?* Newbury Park, CA: Sage.

Bagdikian, B. (2004). *The New Media Monopoly.* Boston: Beacon Press.

Bakardjieva, M. & Smith, R. (2001). The Internet in everyday life: computer networking from the standpoint of the domestic user. *New Media & Society,* 3, 67–83.

Barnett, C. (2004). Neither poison nor cure. In N. Couldry and A. McCarthy (eds.), *MediaSpace: Place, Scale and Culture in a Media Age* (pp. 58–74). London: Routledge.

Bartz, D. (2008). Lawmaker questions Google over privacy practices. *Reuters,* May 21, www.reuters.com/article/internetNews/idUSN2142539620080521 (accessed December 2009).

Bauman, Z. (2000). *Liquid Modernity.* Cambridge: Polity Press.

— (2001). *The Individualized Society.* Cambridge: Polity Press.

— (2005). *Liquid Life.* Cambridge: Polity Press.

— (2007a). *Consuming Life.* Cambridge: Polity Press.

— (2007b). *Liquid Times: Living in an Age of Uncertainty.* Cambridge: Polity Press.

Baym, N. (1995). The emergence of community in computer-mediated communication. In S. G. Jones (ed.), *Cybersociety: Computer-Mediated Communication and Community* (pp. 138–63). Thousand Oaks, CA: Sage.

— (1997). Interpreting soap operas and creating community: inside an electronic fan culture. In S. Kiesler (ed.), *Culture of the Internet* (pp. 103–20). Mahwah, NJ: Erlbaum.

Baym, N., Zhang, Y. B. & Lin, M. C. (2004). Social interactions across media: interpersonal communication on the internet, telephone and face-to-face. *New Media & Society,* 6, 299–318.

Beck, U. (1992). *Risk Society: Towards a New Modernity.* New Delhi: Sage.

(1997). *The Reinvention of Politics. Rethinking Modernity in the Global Social Order.* Cambridge: Polity Press.

(1999). *World Risk Society.* Cambridge: Polity Press.

(2006). *Cosmopolitan Vision.* Cambridge: Polity Press.

Beck, U., Giddens, A. & Lash, S. (1994). *Reflexive Modernization.* Palo Alto, CA: Stanford University Press.

Bell, D. (1981). The information society: the social framework of the information society. In T. Forrester (ed.), *The Microelectronics Revolution* (pp. 500–49). Cambridge, MA: MIT Press.

Benhabib, S. (1992). Models of public space: Hannah Arendt, the Liberal Tradition, and Jurgen Habermas. In C. Calhoun (ed.), *Habermas and the Public Sphere* (pp. 73–98). Cambridge, MA: MIT Press.

Benkler, Y. (2006). *The Wealth of Networks: How Social Production Transforms Markets and Freedom.* New Haven: Yale University Press.

Bimber, B. (1998). The Internet and political transformation: populism, community, and accelerated pluralism. *Polity*, 3, 133–60.

(2000). The study of information technology and civic engagement. *Political Communication*, 17(4), 329–33.

(2001). Information and political engagement in America: the search for effects of information technology at the individual level. *Political Research Quarterly*, 54, 53–67.

Bimber, B. & Davis, R. (2003). *Campaigning Online: The Internet in U.S. Elections.* Oxford: Oxford University Press.

Bird, S. E. (2003). *The Audience in Everyday Life: Living in a Media World.* New York: Routledge.

Blumler, J. G. & Gurevitch, M. (2000). Rethinking the study of political communication. In J. Curran & M. Gurevitch (eds.), *Mass Media and Society* (3rd edn, pp. 155–72). London: Arnold.

(2001). The new media and our political communication discontents: democratizing cyberspace. *Information, Communication & Society*, 4, 1–14.

Bolter, J. D. (1996). Virtual reality and redefinition of self. In L. Strate, R. Jacobson & S. B. Gibson (eds.), *Communication and Cyberspace: Social Interaction in an Electronic Environment* (pp. 105–20). Cresskill, NJ: Hampton Press.

Bolter, J. D. & Brusin, R. (2000). *Remediation: Understanding New Media.* Cambridge, MA: MIT Press.

Boogers, M. & Voerman, G. (2003). Surfing citizens and floating voters: results of an online survey of visitors to political web sites during the Dutch 2002 General Elections. *Information Polity: The International Journal of Government & Democracy in the Information Age*, 8(1/2), 17–27.

Bourdieu, P. (1977). *Outline of a Theory of Practice*. Trans. Richard Nice. Cambridge: Cambridge University Press.

Boutin, P. (2006). A grand unified theory of YouTube and MySpace. *Slate*, posted April 28, 2006, www.slate.com/id/2140635/ (accessed February 2010).

boyd, d. (2004). Friendster and publicly articulated social networks. In *Proceedings of ACM Conference on Human Factors in Computing Systems* (pp. 1279–82). New York: ACM Press.

(2006). Friends, Friendsters, and MySpace Top 8: writing community into being on social network sites. *First Monday*, 11(12), www. firstmonday.org/issues/issue11_12/boyd/ (accessed July 2007).

boyd, d. & Ellison, N. B. (2007). Social network sites: definition, history, and scholarship. *Journal of Computer-Mediated Communication*, 13(1), article 11, http://jcmc.indiana.edu/vol13/issue1/boyd.ellison.html (accessed February 2010).

boyd, d. & Heer, J. (2006). Profiles as conversation: networked identity performance on Friendster. In *Proceedings of the Thirty-Ninth Hawaii International Conference on System Sciences*. Los Alamitos, CA: IEEE Press.

Buckingham, D. (2000). *The Making of Citizens*. London: Routledge.

(2008). Introducing identity. In D. Buckingham (ed.), *Youth, Identity, and Digital Media* (pp. 1–24). Cambridge, MA: MIT Press.

Butler, J. (1990). *Gender Trouble: Feminism and the Subversion of Identity*. New York: Routledge.

Calhoun, C. (1992). *Habermas and the Public Sphere*. Cambridge, MA: MIT Press.

(1997). Nationalism and the public sphere. In J. Weintraub and K. Kumar (eds.), *Public and Private in Thought and Practice* (pp. 75–102). Chicago: University of Chicago Press.

Canclini, N. G. (1995). *Hybrid Cultures: Strategies for Entering and Leaving Modernity*. Minneapolis: University of Minnesota Press.

(2001). *Consumers and Citizens*. Minneapolis: University of Minnesota Press.

(2005). Multicultural policies and integration via the market. In John Hartley (ed.), *Creative Industries* (pp. 93–104). Malden, MA: Blackwell.

Cappella, J. & Jamieson, K. H. (1996). News frames, political cynicism, and media cynicism. *Annals of the American Academy of Political and Social Science*, 546, 71–85.

(1997). *Spiral of Cynicism: The Press and the Public Good*. New York: Oxford University Press.

(2008). *Echo Chamber: Rush Limbaugh and the Conservative Media Establishment*. New York: Oxford University Press.

Cappella, J., Price, V. & Nir, L. (2002). Argument repertoire as a reliable and valid measure of opinion quality: Electronic Dialogue Campaign 2000. *Political Communication*, 19, 73–93.

Carey, J. (1989). *Communication as Culture*. New York: Routledge.

(1995). The press, public opinion, and public discourse. In T. Glasser and C. Salmon (eds.), *Public Opinion and the Communication of Consent* (pp. 373–402). New York: Guilford.

Cassidy, J. (2006). Me media: how hanging out on the Internet became big business. *The New Yorker*, 82 (13, May 15), 50.

Castells, M. (1977). *The Urban Question: A Marxist Approach*. Cambridge, MA: MIT Press.

(2000). *The Rise of the Network Society*. Oxford: Blackwell.

(2001). *The Internet Galaxy*. Oxford: Oxford University Press.

(2009). *Communication Power*. New York: Oxford.

Castells, M., Fernandez-Ardevol, M., Linchuan Qiu, J. & Sey, A. (2006). *Mobile Communication and Society*. Cambridge, MA: MIT Press.

Castoriadis, C. (1975/1987). *The Imaginary Institution of Society*. Trans. Kathleen Blamey, 1987. Cambridge, MA: MIT Press, 1998.

La Brèche: vingt ans après. Paris.

Philosophy, *Politics, Autonomy: Essays in Political Philosophy*. New York: Oxford.

Figures of the Thinkable. Trans.: H. Arnold. Stanford, CA: Stanford University Press.

Chadwick, A. (2007). *Internet Politics: States, Citizens, and New Communication Technologies*. New York: Oxford University Press.

Cohen, L. (2003). *A Consumer's Republic: The Politics of Mass Consumption in Postwar America*. New York: Vintage.

Coleman, S. (2005a). Just how risky is online voting? *Information Polity: The International Journal of Government & Democracy in the Information Age*, 10(1/2), 95–104.

(2005b). The lonely citizen: indirect representation in an age of networks. *Political Communication*, 22(2), 197–214.

Consalvo, M. & Miller, T. (2009). Reinvention through Amnesia. *Critical Studies in Media Communication*, 26(2), 180–90.

Cornfield, M. (2004). Pew Internet project data memo. *Pew Internet & American Life Project*, www.pewinternet.org/pdfs/PIP_Pres_Online_Ads_ Report.pdf (accessed February 2010).

Cornfield, M., Rainie, L. & Horrigan, J. (2003). Untuned keyboards: online campaigners, citizens, and portals in the 2002 elections. *Pew*

Internet & American Life Project, www.pewinternet.org/pdfs/PIP_
Pres_Online_Ads_ Report.pdf (accessed February 2010).

Couldry, N. (2000). *The Place of Media Power: Pilgrims and Witnesses of the Media Age.* London: Routledge.

Couldry, N. & McCarthy, A. (eds.) (2004). *Mediaspace: Place, Scale and Culture in a Media Age.* London: Routledge.

Cox, E. (2002). Making the lucky country. In R. Putnam (ed.), *Democracies in Flux* (pp. 333–58). New York: Oxford University Press.

Curran, J. (1991). Rethinking the media as a public sphere. In P. Dahlgren & C. Sparks (eds.), *Communication and Democracy* (pp. 27–58). London: Routledge.

Dahl, R. A. (1961). *Who Governs? Democracy and Power in an American City.* New Haven: Yale University Press.

Dahlberg, L. (2001). The Internet and democratic discourse: exploring the prospects of online deliberative forums extending the public sphere. *Information, Communication & Society*, 4(4), 615–33.

Dahlgren, P. (1991). Introduction. In P. Dahlgren & C. Sparks (eds.), *Communication and Democracy* (pp. 1–26). London: Routledge.

(2005). The internet, public spheres, and political communication: dispersion and deliberation. *Political Communication*, 22, 147–62.

(2009). *Media and Political Engagement: Citizens, Communication, and Democracy.* New York: Cambridge University Press.

Dahrendorf, R. (1994). The changing quality of citizenship. In B. van Steenbergen (ed.), *The Condition of Citizenship* (pp. 10–19). London: Sage.

Davis, R. (1999). *The Web of Politics: The Internet's Impact on the American Political System.* New York: Oxford.

Dean, K. (2003). *Capitalism and Citizenship: The Impossible Partnership.* London: Routledge.

de Certeau, M. (1984). *The Practice of Everyday Life.* Berkeley: University of California Press.

Deleuze, G. (1998). *Essays Critical and Clinical.* London: Verso.

Delli Carpini, M. X. (1999). In search of the informed citizen: what Americans know about politics and why it matters. Paper presented at the conference on "The Transformation of Civic Life," Middle State Tennessee State University, Murfreesboro and Nashville, Tennessee, November 12–13, 1999.

(2000). Gen.com: youth, civic engagement, and the new information environment. *Political Communication*, 17, 341–9.

Derrida, J. (1992). *The Other Heading: Reflections on Today's Europe.* Trans.

Pascale-Anne Brault and Michael B. Naas. Indianapolis: Indiana University Press.

(1997). *The Politics of Friendship*. London: Verso.

de Sola Pool, I. (1983). *Technologies of Freedom*. Cambridge, MA: Harvard University Press.

de Tocqueville, Alexis (1835/1840). *De la démocratie en Amérique (1835/1840) – Democracy in America*. Trans. and ed. Harvey C. Mansfield and Delba Winthrop. Chicago: University of Chicago Press, 2000.

Deuze, M. (2007). *Media Work*. Cambridge: Polity Press.

Dewey, J. (1927). *The Public and its Problems*. New York: Holt.

Diani, M. (2000). Social movement networks virtual and real. *Information, Communication and Society*, 3(3), 386–401.

DiMaggio, P., Hargittai, E., Celeste, C. & Shafer, S. (2004). Digital inequality: from unequal access to differentiated use. In Kathryn Neckerman (ed.), *Social Inequality* (pp. 355–400). New York: Russell Sage Foundation.

Doctorow, C. (2009). Cyberwar Guide for Iran Elections. *BoingBoing. net*. www.boingboing.net/2009/06/16/cyberwar-guide-for-i.html (accessed June 2009).

Dominick, J. (1999). Who do you think you are? Personal home pages and self-presentation on the world wide web. *Journalism and Mass Communication Quarterly*, 76(4), 646–58.

Donath, J. (1998). Identity and deception in the virtual community. In M. Smith & P. Kollock (eds.), *Communities in Cyberspace* (pp. 29–59). New York: Routledge.

(2007). Signals in social supernets. *Journal of Computer-Mediated Communication*, 13(1), article 12, http://jcmc.indiana.edu/vol13/issue1/donath.html (accessed February 2010).

Donath, J. & boyd, d. (2004). Public displays of connection. *BT Technology Journal*, 22(4), 71.

du Gay, P., Hall, S., Janes, L., Mackay, H. & Negus, K. (1997). *Doing Cultural Studies: The Story of the Sony Walkman*. London: Sage.

Eco, U. (2005). The poetics of the open work. In J. Hartley (ed.), *Creative Industries* (pp. 177–87). New York: Wiley-Blackwell.

Elgesem, D. (1996). Privacy, respect for persons, and risk. In Charles Ess (ed.), *Philosophical Perspectives on Computer-Mediated Communication* (pp. 45–66). Albany: State University of New York Press.

Ellison, N. B., Steinfield, C. & Lampe, C. (2007). The benefits of Facebook "friends": social capital and college students' use of online social network sites. *Journal of Computer-Mediated Communication*, 12(4), article 1, http://jcmc.indiana.edu/vol12/issue4/ellison.html (accessed February 2010).

Elshtain, J. B. (1997). The displacement of politics. In J. Weintraub and K. Kumar (eds.), *Public and Private in Thought and Practice* (pp. 166–81). Chicago: University of Chicago Press.

Ettema, J. S. & Whitney, D. C. (1994). *Audience Making: How the Media Create the Audience*. Thousand Oaks, CA: Sage.

Falk, R. (1994). The making of global citizenship. In B. van Steenbergen (ed.), *The Condition of Citizenship* (pp. 127–40). London: Sage.

Fallows, J. (1996). Why Americans hate the media. *The Atlantic Monthly*, 277(2), February, 45–64.

Farah, B. N. & Higby, M. A. (2001). E-commerce and privacy: conflict and opportunity. *Journal of Education for Business*, 76(6), 303–7.

Foot, K. S. & Schneider, S. M. (2006). *Web Campaigning*. Cambridge, MA: MIT Press.

Foucault, M. (1980). *Power/Knowledge: Selected Interviews and Other Writings, 1972–1977*. Ed. C. Gordon. New York: Pantheon.

Fox, S. (2000). Trust and privacy online: why Americans want to rewrite the rules. *Pew Internet & American Life Project*, August 20, www.pewinternet.org (accessed February 2010).

Fox, S. & Lewis, O. (2001). Fear of online crime: Americans support FBI interception of criminal suspects' email and new laws to protect online privacy. *Pew Internet & American Life Project*, April 2, www.pewinternet.org (accessed February 2010).

Fox, S., Anderson, J. K. & Rainie, L. (2005). The future of the Internet. *Pew Internet & American Life Project*, www.pewinternet.org (accessed June 2009).

Fraser, N. & Gordon, L. (1994). Civil citizenship against social citizenship? In B. van Steenbergen (ed.), *The Condition of Citizenship* (pp. 90–107). London: Sage.

(2008). *Scales of Justice: Reimagining Political Space in a Globalizing World*. Cambridge: Polity Press.

Fraser, N. (1992). Rethinking the public sphere: a contribution to the critique of actually existing democracy. In C. Calhoun (ed.), *Habermas and the Public Sphere* (pp. 109–42). Cambridge, MA: MIT Press.

Gandy, O. H. (1989). The surveillance society: information technology and bureaucratic social control. *Journal of Communication*, 39(3), 61–76.

Gandy, O. H. & Farrall, K. N. (2008). Metaphoric reinforcement of the virtual fence: factors shaping the political economy of property in cyberspace. In A. Chadwick & P. N. Howard (eds.), *The Handbook of Internet Politics* (pp. 349–63). London: Routledge.

Gans, H. (1962). *The Urban Villagers*. New York: Free Press.

(1967). *Levittowners*. New York: Free Press.

Garnham, N. (1990). *Capitalism and Communication: Global Culture and the Economics of Information*. London: Sage.

(2000). *Emancipation, The Media, and Modernity*. Oxford: Oxford University Press.

Geuss, R. (2001). *Public Goods, Private Goods*. Princeton: Princeton University Press.

Giddens, A. (1990). *The Consequences of Modernity*. Cambridge: Polity Press.

Gillis, C. (2002). Soft talk: Hotmail pushes for revenue. *Eastside Journal*, May 16, www.eastsidejournal.com/92560.html (accessed February 2010).

Gillmor, D. (2009). Toward a (new) media literacy in a media saturated world. In Z. Papacharissi (ed.), *Journalism and Citizenship: New Agendas in Communication* (pp. 1–12). New York: Routledge.

Gitelman, L. (2006). *Always Already New*. Cambridge, MA: MIT Press.

Gitlin, T. (1980). *The Whole World is Watching: Mass Media and the Unmaking of the New Left*. Berkeley, CA: University of California Press.

(1983). *Inside Prime Time*. New York: Pantheon Books.

Gobetti, D. (1997). Humankind as a system: private and public agency at the origins of Modern Liberalism. In J. Weintraub and K. Kumar (eds.), *Public and Private in Thought and Practice* (pp. 103–32). Chicago: University of Chicago Press.

Goffman, E. (1959). *The Presentation of Self in Everyday Life*. New York: Doubleday.

(1963). *Behavior in Public Places: Notes on the Social Organization of Gatherings*. New York: Simon & Schuster.

(1971). *Relations in Public: Microstudies of the Public Order*. New York: Basic Books.

Grabe, B. & Bucy, E. (2009). *Image Bite Politics: News and the Visual Framing of Elections*. New York: Oxford.

Gramsci, A. (1971). *Selections from the Prison Notebooks*. New York: International Publishers.

Gross, R. & Acquisti, A. (2005). Information revelation and privacy in online social networks (The Facebook case). In *Proceedings of ACM Workshop on Privacy in the Electronic Society* (pp. 71–80). Alexandria, VA: Association for Computing Machinery.

Grossman, L. K. (1995). *The Electronic Republic.* New York: Viking.

(2009). Iran's protests: why Twitter is the medium of the movement. *Time.com,* www.time.com/time/world/article/0,8599,1905125,00. html (accessed June 2009).

Gunkel, A. H. & Gunkel, D. J. (1997). Virtual geographies: the new worlds of cyberspace. *Critical Studies in Mass Communication,* 14, 123–37.

Gunkel, D. J. & Gunkel, A. H. (2009). Terra Nova 2.0 – The New World of MMORPGs. *Critical Studies in Media Communication,* 26(2), 104–27.

Habermas, J. (1962/1989). *The Structural Transformation of the Public Sphere: An Inquiry into a Category of Bourgeois Society.* Trans. T. Burger and F. Lawrence. Cambridge, MA: MIT Press.

(1973) *Theory and Practice.* Trans. J. Viertel. London: Heinemann.

(1981/1987). *The Theory of Communicative Action,* Vol. II. *Lifeworld and System: A Critique of Functionalist Reason.* Cambridge: Polity Press.

(1991). 'The public sphere'. In C. Mukerji and M. Schudson (eds.), *Rethinking Popular Culture: Contemporary Perspectives in Cultural Studies* (pp. 398–404). Berkeley: University of California Press.

(1992). Further reflections on the Public Sphere. In C. Calhoun (ed.), *Habermas and the Public Sphere* (pp. 421–61). Cambridge, MA: MIT Press.

(1994). Citizenship and national identity. In B. van Steenbergen (ed.), *The Condition of Citizenship* (pp. 20–35). London: Sage.

(2004). *The Divided West.* Malden, MA: Polity Press.

Hague, B. & Loader, B. (1999). *Digital Democracy: Discourse and Decision Making in the Information Age* (pp. 23–38). New York: Routledge.

Halavais, A. (2009). Do dugg Diggers Digg diligently? *Information, Communication & Society,* 12(3), 444–59.

Hall P. A. (2002). The role of government and the distribution of social capital. In R. Putnam (ed.), *Democracies in Flux* (pp. 21–58). New York: Oxford University Press.

Hamelink, C. J. (2000). *The Ethics of Cyberspace.* London: Sage.

Hampton, K. (2002). Place-based and IT mediated "community." *Planning Theory and Practice,* 3(2), 228–31.

Hampton, K. & Wellman, B. (2001a). Long distance community in the network society – contact and support beyond Netville. *American Behavioral Scientist,* 45(3), 476–95.

(2001b). The not so global village. In B. Wellman & C. Haythornwaite (eds.), *The Internet in Everyday Life* (pp. 345–71). Oxford: Blackwell Publishing.

(2003). Neighboring in Netville: how the Internet supports community and social capital in a wired suburb. *City & Community*. 2(4), 277–311.

Hands, J. (2006). Civil society, cosmopolitics and the net: the legacy of 15 February 2003. *Information, Communication & Society*, 9(2), 225–43.

Hanisch, Carol (1969). The personal is political, http://carolhanisch.org/CHwritings/PIP.html (accessed February 2010).

Haraway, D. J. (1991). *Simians, Cyborgs, and Women: The Reinvention of Nature*. New York: Routledge.

Hardy, B. W. & Scheufele, D. A. (2005). The differential gains from Internet use: comparing the moderating role of talk and online interactions. *Journal of Communication*, 55, 71–84.

Hargittai, E. (2007). Whose space? Differences among users and non-users of social network sites. *Journal of Computer-Mediated Communication*, 13(1), article 14, http://jcmc.indiana.edu/vol13/issue1/hargittai.html (accessed February 2010).

(2008). The digital reproduction of inequality. In David Grusky (ed.), *Social Stratification* (pp. 936–44). Boulder, CO: Westview Press.

Hart, R. P. (1994). Easy citizenship: television's curious legacy. *Annals of the American Academy of Political and Social Science*, 546, 109–20.

Hartley, J. (2000). Communicative democracy in redactional society: the future of journalism studies. *Journalism*, 1(1), 39–48.

(2005). Creative industries. In J. Hartley (ed.), *Creative Industries* (pp. 1–40). New York: Wiley-Blackwell.

Hassan, R. (2008). *The Information Society*. Cambridge: Polity Press.

Hay, J. (2003). Unaided virtues: the (neo-)liberalization of the domestic sphere and the new architecture of community. In J. Bratich, J. Packer & C. McCarthy (eds.), *Foucault, Cultural Studies, and Governmentality* (pp. 165–206). Albany, NY: State University of New York Press.

Hay, J. S., Grossberg, L. & Wartella, E. (1996). *The Audience and its Landscape*. Boulder, CO: Westview Press.

Haythornthwaite, C. (2000). Online personal networks: size, composition and media use among distance learners. *New Media and Society*, 2(2), 195–226.

(2001). The internet in everyday life. *American Behavioral Scientist*, 45(3), 363–82.

(2002a). Strong, weak, and latent ties and the impact of new media. *Information Society*, 18(5), 385–401.

(2002b). Building social networks via computer networks: creating and sustaining distributed learning communities. In K. A. Renninger

& W. Shumar (eds.), *Building Virtual Communities: Learning and Change in Cyberspace* (pp. 159–90). Cambridge: Cambridge University Press.

(2005). Social networks and internet connectivity effects. *Information Communication & Society*, 8(2), 125–47.

Haythornthwaite, C. & Wellman, B. (1998). Work, Friendship and media use for information exchange in a networked organization. *Journal of the American Society for Information Science*, 49(12), 1101–14.

Haythornthwaite, C., Wellman, B. & Mantei, M. (1995). Work relationships and media use: a social network analysis. *Group Decision and Negotiation*, 4(3), 193–211.

Heater, D. (2004). *A Brief History of Citizenship*. New York: New York University Press.

Hebdige, D. (1993). Redeeming witness: in the tracks of the Homeless Vehicle Project. *Cultural Studies*, 7(2), 173–223.

Heffernan, V. (2007). The many tribes of YouTube. *New York Times*, May 27, pp. 1, 23, Section 2.

Heidegger, M. (1954/1977). *The Question concerning Technology and Other Essays*. New York: Harper & Row.

(1962). *Being and Time*. Trans. J. Macquarrie & E. Robinson. New York: Harper and Row.

Herbst, S. (1993). *Numbered Voices: How Opinion Polling Has Shaped American Politics*. Chicago: University of Chicago Press.

Herbst, S., O'Keefe, G., Shapiro, R. Y., Lindeman, M. & Glynn, C. (2004). *Public Opinion*. Boulder, CO: Westview.

Herring, S. C., Kouper, I., Paolillo, J. C., et al. (2005). Conversations in the blogosphere: an analysis "From the bottom up." *BROG: The (We) Blog Research on Genre Project*, www.blogninja.com/ (accessed June 2005).

Herring, S. C., Kouper, I., Scheidt, L. A. & Wright, E. (2004). Women and children last: The discursive construction of weblogs. In L. Gurak et al. (eds.), *Into the Blogosphere: Rhetoric, Community, and Culture of Weblogs*, http://blog.lib.umn.edu/blogosphere/women_and_children.html (accessed February 2010).

Hesse, H. (1930/1968). *Narcissus and Goldmund*. New York: Macmillan.

Hill, K. A. & Hughes, J. E. (1998). *Cyberpolitics: Citizen Activism in the Age of the Internet*. New York: Rowman and Littlefield Publishers, Inc.

Howard, P. (2006). *New Media Campaigns and the Managed Citizen*. New York: Cambridge University Press.

Howard, P. and Jones, S. (eds.) (2004). *Society Online: The Internet in Context*. Thousand Oaks, CA: Sage.

Huffington Post (June 17, 2009). Iran protests 2009: HuffPost bloggers weigh in on political fallout, Twitter and what happens next. *HuffingtonPost.com*, www.huffingtonpost.com/2009/06/17/iran-protests-2009-huffpo_n_216870.html (accessed June 2009).

Humphreys, L. (2005). Cell phones in public: social interactions in a wireless era. *New Media & Society*, 7, 810–33.

Hutchby, I. (2001). *Conversation and Technology: From the Telephone to the Internet*. Cambridge: Polity Press.

Inglehart, R. & Welzel, C. (2005). *Modernization, Cultural Change and Democracy*. Cambridge: Cambridge University Press.

Inoguchi, T. (2002). Broadening the basis of social capital in Japan. In R. Putnam (ed.), *Democracies in Flux* (pp. 359–92). New York: Oxford University Press.

Ito, J. (2003). *Weblogs and Emergent Democracy*, http://joi.ito.com/static/emergentdemocracy.html (accessed December 3, 2008).

Jamieson, K. (2003). *The Press Effect*. New York: Oxford University Press.

Jankowski, N. W. & van Selm, M. (2000). The promise and practice of public debate in cyberspace. In K. Hacker & J. van Dijk (eds.), *Digital Democracy: Issues of Theory and Practice* (pp. 1–9). London: Sage.

Jenkins, H. (1992). *Textual Poachers: Television Fans and Participatory Culture*. New York: Routledge.

(2006a). *Convergence Culture: Where Old and New Media Collide*. New York: New York University Press.

(2006b). *Fans, Bloggers and Gamers: Media Consumers in a Digital Age*. New York: New York University Press.

Jennings, M. K. & Zeitner, V. (2003). Internet use and civic engagement: a longitudinal analysis. *Public Opinion Quarterly*, 67, 311–34.

Jensen, K. B. (2009). Three step flow. *Journalism*, 10, 335–7.

Jensen, J. L. (2003). Public spheres on the Internet: anarchic or government-sponsored – a comparison. *Scandinavian Political Studies*, 26(4), 349–74.

Jensen, M. J., Danziger, J. N. & Venkatesh, A. (2007). Civil society and cyber society: the role of the Internet in community associations and democratic politics. *The Information Society*, 23(1), 39–50.

Jhally, S. (1990). *The Codes of Advertising*. London: Routledge.

Johnson, B. (2007). Facebook v. MySpace: a class divide. *The Guardian*, June 26, p. 19, www.guardian.co.uk/world/2007/jun/26/usa.news (accessed May 15, 2008).

Johnson, T. J. & Kaye, B. K. (1998). A vehicle for engagement or a haven for the disaffected? Internet use, political alienation, and voter participation. In T. J. Johnson, C. E. Hays & S. P. Hays (eds.),

Engaging the Public: How the Government and Media can Reinvigorate Democracy (pp. 123–35). Lanham, MD: Roman and Littlefield.

Jones, S. (1997a). The Internet and its social landscape. In S. Jones (ed.), *Virtual Culture: Identity and Communication in Cybersociety* (pp. 7–35). Thousand Oaks, CA: Sage.

(ed.) (1997b). *CyberSociety 2.0: Revisiting CMC and Community.* Thousand Oaks, CA: Sage.

(ed.) (1998). *Virtual Culture: Identity and Communication in Cybersociety.* Thousand Oaks, CA: Sage.

Jordan, T. (2008). *Hacking.* Cambridge: Polity Press.

Kaid, L. L. (2002). Political advertising and information seeking: comparing exposure via traditional and Internet channels. *Journal of Advertising,* 31, 27–35.

Katz, J. E. & Rice, R. E. (2002). *Social Consequences of Internet Use: Access, Involvement and Interaction.* Cambridge, MA: MIT Press.

Kaye, B. K. (2007). Blog use motivations. In M. Tremayne (ed)., *Blogging, Citizenship, and the Future of Media* (pp. 127–48). New York: Routledge.

Keane, J. (1991). *The Media and Democracy.* London: Wiley-Blackwell.

Keenan, T. (1993). Windows: of vulnerability. In B. Robbins (ed.), *The Phantom Public Sphere* (pp. 121–41). Minneapolis: Minnesota University Press.

Kenix, L. (2007). In search of Utopia: an analysis of non-profit web pages. *Information, Communication & Society,* 10(1), 69–94.

Kerbel, M. R. & Bloom, J. D. (2005). Blog for America and civic involvement. *Harvard International Journal of Press Politics,* 10(4), 3–27.

Kivisto, P. & Faist, T. (2007). *Citizenship: Discourse, Theory, and Transnational Prospects.* New York: Wiley.

Kling, R. (1996). Hopes and horrors: technological utopianism and anti-utopianism in narratives of computerization. In R. Kling (ed.), *Computerization and Controversy* (pp. 40–58). Boston: Academic Press.

Kobayashi, T., Ikeda, K. & Miyata, K. (2006). Social capital online: collective use of the Internet and reciprocity as lubricants of democracy. *Communication & Society,* 9(5), 582–611.

Kohut, A. (2003). Perceptions of partisan bias seen as growing, especially by Democrats: cable and Internet loom large in fragmented political news universe. *Pew Internet & American Life Project,* www. pewinternet.org/pdfs/ PIP_Pres_Online_Ads_ Report.pdf (accessed January 2005).

(2008). Key news audiences now blend online and traditional sources: audience segments in a changing news environment. *Pew Research Center for the People & the Press*, http://people-press.org/report/444/news-media (accessed June 2009).

Kondylis, P. (1991). *Der Niedergang der bürgerlichen Denk- und Lebensformen. Die liberale Moderne und die massendemokratische Postmoderne* [The Decline of the Bourgeois Forms of Thinking and Living]. Weinheim: VCH-Verlagsgesellschaft.

Kraut, R., Kiesler, S., Boneva, K., Cummings, J., Helgeson, J. & Crawford, A. (2002). Internet paradox revisited. *Journal of Social Issues*, 58(1), 49–74.

Kraut, R., Patterson, M., Lundmark, V., Kiesler, S., Mukophadhyay, T. & Scherlis, W. (1998). Internet paradox: a social technology that reduces social involvement and psychological well-being? *American Psychologist*, 53, 1017–31.

Krugman, P. (2008). The Gramm connection. *The New York Times.com*, March 29 http://krugman.blogs.nytimes.com/2008/03/29/the-gramm-connection/ (accessed December 2009).

Kulikova, S. V. & Perlmutter, D. D. (2007). Blogging down the dictator? The Kyrgyz Revolution and Samizdat websites. *International Communication Gazette*, 69(1), 29–50.

Kumar, K. (1997). Home: the promise and predicament of private life at the end of the twentieth century. In J. Weintraub and K. Kumar (eds.), *Public and Private in Thought and Practice* (pp. 204–36). Chicago: University of Chicago Press.

Laclau, E. (1991). *New Reflections on the Revolution of Our Time*. London: Verso.

Lange, P. G. (2007). Publicly private and privately public: social networking on YouTube. *Journal of Computer-Mediated Communication*, 13(1), article 18, http://jcmc.indiana.edu/vol13/issue1/lange.html (accessed February 2010).

Langman, L. (2005). From virtual public spheres to global justice: a critical theory of internetworked social movements. *Sociological Theory*, 23(1), 42–74.

LaRose, R., Eastin, M. S. & Gregg, J. (2001). Reformulating the Internet paradox: social cognitive explanations of Internet use and depression. *Journal of Online Behavior*, 1(2), www.behavior.net/JOB/v1n2/paradox.html (accessed February 2010).

Lasch, C. (1977). *Haven in a Heartless World: The Family Besieged*. New York: Basic.

(1979). *The Culture of Narcissism*. New York: Norton & Co.

Lazarsfeld, P., Gaudet, H. & Berelson, B. F. (1944). *The People's Choice.* New York: Columbia University Press.

Lee, Laurie Thomas (2000). Privacy, security and intellectual property. In Alan B. Albarran & David H. Goff (eds.), *Understanding the Web: Social, Political, and Economic Dimensions of the Internet* (pp. 135–64). Arnes: Iowa State University Press.

Lefebvre, H. (1974/1991). *The Production of Space.* Trans. D. Nicholson-Smith. Oxford: Blackwell.

Lessig, L. (1999). *Code: And Other Laws of Cyberspace.* New York: Basic Books.

(2005). *Free Culture.* New York: Penguin.

Lii, D. (1998). Social spheres and public life: a structural origin. *Theory, Culture & Society*, 15(2), 115–35.

Ling, R. & Donner, J. (2009). *Mobile Communication.* Cambridge: Polity Press.

Lippmann, W. (1922). *Public Opinion.* New Brunswick: Transaction Publishers.

(1925). *The Phantom Public.* New Brunswick: Transaction Publishers.

Liu, H. (2007). Social network profiles as taste performances. *Journal of Computer-Mediated Communication*, 13(1), article 13, http://jcmc.indiana.edu/vol13/issue1/liu.html (accessed February 2010).

Liu, H., Maes, P. & Davenport, G. (2006). Unraveling the taste fabric of social networks. *International Journal on Semantic Web and Information Systems*, 2(1), 42–71.

Livingstone, S. (2005). In defense of privacy: mediating the public/private boundary at home. *Changing Media, Changing Europe*, 2, 163–85.

Locke, C., Levine, R., Searls, D. & Weinberger, D. (2001). *The Cluetrain Manifesto: Business as Usual.* New York: Basic.

Lyotard, J. F. (1984). *The Postmodern Condition.* Minneapolis: University of Minnesota Press.

Machlup, F. (1962). *The Production and Distribution of Knowledge in the United States.* Princeton, NJ: Princeton University Press.

MacKinnon, C. A. (1987). *Feminism Unmodified: Discourses on Life and Law.* Cambridge, MA: Harvard University Press.

(1989). *Toward a Feminist Theory of the State.* Cambridge, MA: Harvard University Press.

Malina, A. (1999). Perspectives on citizen democratization and alienation in the virtual public sphere. In B. Hague & B. Loader, *Digital Democracy: Discourse and Decision Making in the Information Age* (pp. 23–38). New York: Routledge.

Mancini, P. (1991). The public sphere and the use of news in a "coalition" system of government. In P. Dahlgren & C. Sparks (eds.), *Communication and Democracy* (pp. 137–54). London: Routledge.

Manovich, L. (2001) *The Language of New Media*. Cambridge. MA: MIT Press. (2005). Remix and remixability. *New Media Fix,* http://newmediafix. net/daily/?p=204 (accessed April 2009).

Maramotti, L. (2005). Connecting creativity. In J. Hartley (ed.), *Creative Industries* (pp. 205–13). New York: Wiley-Blackwell.

Marcella, R., Baxter, G. & Moore, N. (2002). An exploration of the effectiveness for the citizen of Web-based systems of communicating UK parliamentary and devolved assembly information. *Journal of Government Information,* 29(6), 371–91.

Margolis, M. & Resnick, D. (2000). *Politics as Usual: The Cyberspace Revolution*. Thousand Oaks, CA: Sage.

Margolis, M., Resnick, D. & Tu, C. (1997). Campaigning on the Internet: parties and candidates on the World Wide Web in the 1996 primary season. *Harvard International Journal of Press/Politics,* 2, 59–78.

Marshall, T. H. & Bottomore, T. (1992). *Citizenship and Social Class*. London: Pluto Press.

Marvin, C. (1990). *When Old Technologies Were New: Thinking about Electric Communication in the Late Nineteenth Century*. New York: Oxford.

May, C. (2008). Globalizing the logic of openness: open sources software and the global governance of intellectual property. In A. Chadwick & P. N. Howard (eds.), *The Handbook of Internet Politics* (pp. 364–75). London: Routledge.

McCarthy, A. (2001). *Ambient Television*. Durham: Duke University Press.

McChesney, R. (1995). The Internet and U.S. communication policy-making in historical and critical perspective. *Journal of Computer-Mediated Communication,* 1(4), www.usc.edu/dept/ annenberg/vol1/issue4/mcchesney.html# Democracy (accessed January 2001).

(2004). *The Problem of the Media: US Communication Politics in the Twenty-First Century*. New York: The Monthly Review Press.

(2008). *Communication Revolution: Critical Junctures and the Future of Media*. New York: The New Press.

McConnell, B. & Huba, J. (2006). *Citizen Marketers: where People are the Message*. Chicago: Dearborn Trade.

McKenna, A. (2001). Playing fair with consumer privacy in the global on-line environment. *Information & Communications Technology Law,* 10(3), 339–54.

Meikle, G. (2005). Open publishing, open technology. In John Hartley (ed.), *Creative Industries* (pp. 70–82). Malden, MA: Blackwell.

Melucci, A. (1994). A strange kind of newness: what's "New" in new social movements? In *New Social Movements: From Ideology to Identity* (pp. 101–30). Philadelphia: Temple University Press.

(1996). *Challenging Codes: Collective Action in the Information Age*. New York: Cambridge University Press.

(1999). Difference and otherness in a global society. In M. Bulmer & J. Solomos (eds.), *Racism* (pp. 412–25). Oxford: Oxford University Press.

Mendelson, A. & Papacharissi, Z. (2010). Look at us: collective narcissism in college student Facebook photo galleries. In Z. Papacharissi (ed.), *The Networked Self: Identity, Connectivity and Culture on Social Network Sites*. New York: Routledge.

Meraz, S. (2007). Analyzing political conversation on the Howard Dean candidate blog. In M. Tremayne (ed)., *Blogging, Citizenship, and the Future of Media* (pp. 59–82). New York: Routledge.

(2009). The many faced "you" of social media. In Z. Papacharissi (ed.), *Journalism and Citizenship: New Agendas in Communication* (pp. 123–48). New York: Routledge.

Meyrowitz, J. (1986). *No Sense of Place*. New York: Oxford.

Miessen, M. (2007). Articulated power relations: Markus Miessen in conversation with Chantal Mouffe. *Roundtable: Research Architecture*, http://roundtable.kein.org/node/545 (accessed April 2009).

Miller, T. (2007). *Cultural Citizenship: Cosmopolitanism, Consumerism, and Television in a Neoliberal Age*. Philadelphia: Temple University Press.

Miller, T., Govil, N., McMurria, J. & Maxwell, R. (2005). Conclusion to global Hollywood. In John Hartley (ed.), *Creative Industries* (pp. 147–56). Malden, MA: Blackwell.

Mills, C. W. (1953). *White Collar: The American Middle Classes*. New York: Oxford University Press.

(1956). *The Power Elite*. New York: Oxford University Press.

Mitra, A. (1997a). Virtual community: looking for India on the Internet. In S. G. Jones (ed.), *Virtual Culture: Identity and Communication in Cybersociety* (pp. 55–79). Thousand Oaks, CA: Sage.

(1997b). Diasporic web sites: ingroup and outgroup discourse. *Critical Studies in Mass Communication*, 14, 158–81.

Montgomery, K. (2009). *Generation Digital: Politics, Commerce, and Childhood in the Age of the Internet*. Cambridge, MA: MIT Press.

Montgomery. K. & Gottlieb-Robbles, B. (2006). Youth as e-citizens: the Internet's contribution to civic engagement. In D. Buckingham &

R. Willett (eds.), *Digital Generations: Children, Young People, and New Media* (pp. 131–48). Mahwah, NJ: LEA.

Moores, S. (2004). The doubling of place: electronic media, time–space arrangements and social relationships. In N. Couldry and A. McCarthy (eds)., *Mediaspace: Place, Scale and Culture in a Media Age* (pp. 21–36). London: Routledge.

Morley, D. (2000). *Home Territories: Media, Mobility and Identity*. London: Routledge.

(2007). *Media, Modernity and Technology: The Geography of the New*. London: Routledge.

Mosco, V. (2004). *The Digital Sublime: Myth, Power, and Cyberspace*. Cambridge, MA: MIT Press.

Mossberger, K., Tolbert, C. J. & McNeal, R. S. (2007). *Digital Citizenship: The Internet, Society, and Participation*. Cambridge, MA: MIT Press.

Mouffe, C. (2000). *The Democratic Paradox*. London: Verso.

(2005). *On the Political*. London: Routledge.

Moy, P., Manosevitch, E., Stamm, K. & Dunsmore, K. (2005). Linking dimensions of internet use and civic engagement. *Journalism and Mass Communication Quarterly*, 82(3), 571–86.

Mumford, L. (1934). *Technics and Civilization*. New York: Harcourt, Brace & Company.

Murray, J. H. (2005). Digital TV and the emerging formats of cyberdrama. In J. Hartley (ed.), *Creative Industries* (pp. 188–98). New York: Wiley-Blackwell.

Negroponte, N. (1998). Beyond digital. *Wired*, 6(12), 288.

Newhagen, J. E. & Rafaeli, S. (1996). Why communication researchers should study the Internet: a dialogue. *Journal of Communication*, 46(1), 4–13.

Noam, E. M. (2005). Why the Internet is bad for democracy. *Communications of the ACM*, 48(10), 57–8.

Norris, P. (2009). Who surfs? New technology, old voters and virtual democracy. In E. C. Kamarck & J. S. Nye, Jr. (eds.), *Democracy.com* (pp. 71–94). New Hampshire: Hollis.

Offe, C. & Fuchs, S. (2002). A decline of social capital? In R. Putnam (ed.), *Democracies in Flux* (pp. 189–244). New York: Oxford University Press.

O'Loughlin, B. (2001). The political implications of digital innovations: trade-offs of democracy and liberty in the developed world. *Information, Communication & Society*, 4(4), 595–614.

Ong, A. (1999). *Flexible Citizenship*. Durham, NC: Duke University Press.

Paletta, D. & Scannell, K. (2009). Ten questions for those fixing the financial mess. *The Wall Street Journal*, March 10, A10.

Papacharissi, Z. (2002a). The self online: the utility of personal home pages. *Journal of Broadcasting & Electronic Media*, 46(3), 346–68.

(2002b). The presentation of self in virtual life: characteristics of personal home pages. *Journalism and Mass Communication Quarterly*, 79(3), 643–60.

(2002c). The virtual sphere: the Internet as the public sphere. *New Media & Society*, 4(1), 5–23.

(2007). The blogger revolution? Audiences as media producers. In M. Tremayne (ed.), *Blogging, Citizenship, and the Future of Media* (pp. 21–38). New York: Routledge.

(2008). The virtual sphere 2.0: the Internet, the public sphere and beyond. In Andrew Chadwick & Philip Howard (eds.), *The Handbook of Internet Politics* (pp. 230–45). London: Routledge.

(2009). The virtual geographies of social networks: a comparative analysis of Facebook, LinkedIn and ASmallWorld. *New Media & Society*, 11(1–2), 199–220.

Papacharissi, Z. & Fernback, J. (2008). The aesthetic power of the Fab 5: discussing themes of homochromativity in *Queer Eye for the Straight Guy*. *Journal of Communication Inquiry*, 32(4), 348–67.

Papacharissi, Z. & Mendelson, A. (2008). Toward a new(er) sociability: uses, gratifications, and social capital on Facebook. Paper presented to the Association of Internet Researcher, Copenhagen, October.

Papacharissi, Z. & Rubin, A. M. (2000). Predictors of Internet use. *Journal of Broadcasting & Electronic Media*, 44, 175–96.

Pateman, C. (1989). *The Disorder of Women*. Stanford: Stanford University Press.

Patterson, T. (1993). *Out of Order*. New York: Knopf.

(1996). Bad news, bad governance. *Annals of the American Academy of Political and Social Science*, 546, 97–108.

Pavlik, J. V. (1994). Citizen access, involvement, and freedom of expression in an electronic environment. In F. Williams & J. V. Pavlik (eds.), *The People's Right to Know: Media, Democracy, and the Information Highway* (pp. 139–62). Hillsdale, NJ: Lawrence Erlbaum.

Pérez-Díaz, V. (2002). Social capital in Spain from the 1930s to the 1990s. In R. Putnam (ed.), *Democracies in Flux* (pp. 245–88). New York: Oxford University Press.

Phillips, D. J. (2008). Locational surveillance: embracing the patterns of our lives. In A. Chadwick & P. N. Howard (eds.), *The Handbook of Internet Politics* (pp. 337–48). London: Routledge.

Pickard, V. W. (2006). Assessing the radical democracy of Indymedia: discursive, technical and institutional constructions. *Critical Studies in Media Communication*, 23(1), 19–38.

Pocock, J. G. A. (1995). The ideal of citizenship since classical times. In R. Beiner (ed.), *Theorizing Citizenship*. Albany, NY: SUNY Press.

Poster, M. (1995). The Internet as a public sphere?, *Wired*, 3(1), 209.

Poulantzas, N. (1978). *State, Power, Socialism*. London: Verso.

Putnam, R. (1996). The strange disappearance of civic America. *The American Prospect*, 24(1), 34–48.

(2001). *Bowling Alone: The Collapse and Revival of American Community*. New York: Simon & Schuster.

(2002). *Democracies in Flux*. New York: Oxford University Press.

Rainie, L. (2008). Changing news audience behavior. *Pew Internet & American Life Project*, www.pewinternet.org/Commentary/2008/August/Changing-news-audience-behavior.aspx (accessed June 2009).

Rash, W., Jr. (1997). *Politics on the Nets: Wiring the Political Process*. New York: W. H. Freeman.

Reilly, R. A. (1999). Conceptual foundations of privacy: looking backward before stepping forward. *The Richmond Journal of Law and Technology*, 6(2), www.richmond.edu/jolt/v6i2/article1.html (accessed February 2010).

Rheingold, H. (1993). *The Virtual Community*. Reading, MA: Addison-Wesley Publishing Company.

(2002). *Smart Mobs: The Next Social Revolution*. New York: Basic.

Riesman, D. (1950). *The Lonely Crowd*. New Haven: Yale University Press.

Robbins, B. (1993). *The Phantom Public Sphere*. Minneapolis: University of Minnesota Press.

(1998). Actually existing cosmopolitanism. In P. Cheah & B. Robbins (eds.), *Cosmopolitics* (pp. 1–19). Minneapolis: University of Minnesota Press.

Robins, K. & Webster, F. (1999). *Times of the Technoculture*. London: Routledge.

Robinson, S. (2009). "Searching for my own unique place in the story": a comparison of journalistic and citizen-produced coverage of Hurricane Katrina's anniversary. In Z. Papacharissi (ed.), *Journalism and Citizenship: New Agendas in Communication* (pp. 166–88). New York: Routledge.

Roscoe, J. (2005). Performing the "Real" 24/7. In J. Hartley (ed.), *Creative Industries* (pp. 214–18). New York: Wiley-Blackwell.

Ross, A. (2004). Dot.com urbanism. In N. Couldry and A. McCarthy (eds.), *MediaSpace: Place, Scale and Culture in a Media Age* (pp. 145–63). London: Routledge.

Rothstein, B. (2002). Social capital in the social democratic state. In R. Putnam (ed.), *Democracies in Flux* (pp. 289–332). New York: Oxford University Press.

Rutigliano, L. (2009). Mapping citizen coverage of the dual city. In Z. Papacharissi (ed.), *Journalism and Citizenship: New Agendas in Communication* (pp. 189–205). New York: Routledge.

Salter, L. (2005). Colonization tendencies in the development of the world wide web. *New Media & Society*, 7(3), 291–309.

Sassi, S. (2000). The controversies of the Internet and the revitalization of local political life. In K. L. Hacker & J. van Dijk (eds.), *Digital Democracy* (pp. 90–104). London: Sage.

  (2005). Cultural differentiation or social segregation? Four approaches to the digital divide. *New Media Society*, 7(5), 684–700.

Scammell, M. (2000). The Internet and civic engagement: the age of the citizen-consumer. *Political Communication*, 17(4), 351–55.

Scannell, P. (1996). *Radio, Television and Modern Life: A Phenomenological Approach*. Oxford: Blackwell.

Scheufele, D. A. & Nisbet, M. (2002). Being a citizen online: new opportunities and dead ends. *Harvard International Journal of Press/Politics*, 7, 55–75.

Schement, J. R. & Curtis, T. (1997). *Tendencies and Tensions of the Information Age*. New Brunswick, NJ: Transaction Publishers.

Schement, J. R. & Lievrouw, L. A. (eds.) (1987). *Competing Visions, Complex Realities: Social Aspects of the Information Society*. Norwood, NJ: Ablex.

  (1989). A third vision: capitalism and the industrial origins of the information society. In J. R. Schement & L. A. Lievrouw (eds.) (1989). *Competing Visions, Complex Realities: Social Aspects of the Information Society* (pp. 33–45). Norwood, NJ: Ablex.

Schiller, D. (2000). *Digital Capitalism*. Cambridge, MA: MIT Press.

  (2006). *How to Think About Information*. Urbana: University of Illinois Press.

Schmitz, J. (1997). Structural relations, electronic media, and social change: the public electronic network and the homeless. In S. G. Jones (ed.), *Virtual Culture: Identity and Communication in Cybersociety* (pp. 80–101). Thousand Oaks, CA: Sage.

Schudson, M. (1997) Why conversation is not the soul of democracy. *Critical Studies in Mass Communication*, 14, 1–13.

(1998). *The Good Citizen: A History of American Civic Life.* New York: Free Press.

Schwarzmantel, J. (2003). *Citizenship and Identity: Towards a New Republic.* London: Routledge.

Scott, T. D. (2007). Analyzing political conversation on the Howard Dean candidate blog. In M. Tremayne (ed.), *Blogging, Citizenship, and the Future of Media* (pp. 39–58). New York: Routledge.

Semetko, H. A. & Krasnoboka, N. (2003). The political role of the internet in societies in transition. *Party Politics,* 9(1), 77–104.

Sender, K. (2001). Gay readers, consumers and a dominant gay habitus: 25 years of the *Advocate* magazine. *Journal of Communication,* 51(1), 73–99.

Sennett, R. (1970). *The Uses of Disorder.* New York: W. W. Norton.

(1974). *The Fall of Public Man.* New York: Random House.

(2006). *The Culture of the New Capitalism.* New Haven: Yale University Press.

Shah, D. V., Cho, J., Eveland Jr., W. P., & Kwak, N. (2005). Information and expression in a digital age: modeling Internet effects on civic participation. *Communication Research,* 32(5), 531–65.

Shah, D. V., Kwak, N. & Holbert, R. L. (2001). Connecting and disconnecting with civic life: patterns of Internet use and the production of social capital. *Political Communication,* 18, 141–62.

Shapiro, C. & Varian, H. R. (1998). *Information Rules: A Strategic Guide to the Network Economy.* Cambridge, MA: Harvard Business School Press.

Silver, A. (1997). "Two different sorts of commerce" – friendship and strangership in civil society. In J. Weintraub and K. Kumar (eds.), *Public and Private in Thought and Practice* (pp. 43–74). Chicago: University of Chicago Press.

Silverstone, R. (2007). *Media and Morality: On the Rise of the Mediapolis.* Cambridge: Polity Press.

Silverstone, R. & Hirsch, E. (1992). *Consuming Technologies: Media and Information in Domestic Spaces.* London: Routledge.

Simone, Maria (2006). CODEPINK alert: mediated citizenship in the public sphere. *Social Semiotics,* 16(2), 345–64.

Skocpol, T. (2002). From membership to advocacy. In R. Putnam (ed.), *Democracies in Flux* (pp. 103–36). New York: Oxford University Press.

Slotnik, D. E. (2007). Too few friends? A web site lets you buy some (and they're hot). *The New York Times,* February 26 from www.nytimes.com/2007/02/26/technology/26fake.html (accessed May 15, 2008).

Spigel, L. (1994). *Make Room for TV: Television and the Family Ideal in Postwar America*. Chicago: University of Chicago Press.

(2001). *Welcome to the Dreamhouse: Popular Media and Postwar Suburbs*. Durham, NC: Duke University Press.

Story, L. (2007). Putting amateurs in charge. *New York Times*, May 26, pp. B1, B9.

Sullivan, A. (2002). An honest blogger will never make a quick buck. *Sunday Times*, October 13, p. A4.

Sundar, S. S., Edwards, H. H., Hu, Y. & Stavrositu. C. (2007). Blogging for better health: putting the "public" back in public health. In M. Tremayne (ed.), *Blogging, Citizenship, and the Future of Media* (pp. 83–102). New York: Routledge.

Sunstein, C. (2001). *Republic.com*. Princeton: Princeton University Press.

Swanson, D. (2000). The homologous evolution of political communication and civic engagement: good news, bad news, and no news. *Political Communication*, 17(4), 409–14.

Thompson, J. (1995). *The Media and Modernity: A Social Theory of the Media*. Palo Alto, CA: Stanford University Press.

(2000). *Political Scandal: Power and Visibility in the Media Age*. Cambridge: Polity Press.

Toffler, A. (1980). *The Third Wave*. New York: Bantam.

Tremayne, M. (ed.) (2007). *Blogging, citizenship, and the Future of Media*. New York: Routledge.

Turkle, S. (1984). *The Second Self: Computers and the Human Spirit*. New York: Simon & Schuster.

(1995). *Life on the Screen: Identity in the Age of the Internet*. New York: Simon & Schuster.

(1996). Parallel lives: working on identity in virtual space. In D. Grodin & T. R. Lindlof (eds.), *Constructing the Self in a Mediated World: Inquiries in Social Construction* (pp. 156–75). Thousand Oaks, CA: Sage.

(1997). Constructions and reconstructions of self in virtual reality: playing in the MUDs. In S. Kiesler (ed.), *Culture of the Internet* (pp. 143–55). Mahwah, NJ: Erlbaum.

Turow, J. (2001). Family boundaries, commercialism, and the Internet: a framework for research. *Journal of Applied Developmental Psychology*, 22(1), 73–86.

Uslaner, E. M. (2004). Trust, civic engagement, and the Internet. *Political Communication*, 21(2), 223–42.

van Aelst, P. & Walgrave, S. (2002). New media, new movements? The role of the internet in shaping the "anti-globalization" movement. *Information, Communication & Society*, 5(4), 465–93.

van Dijk, J. (1999). *The Network Society: Social Aspects of New Media.* London: Sage.

van Steenbergen, B. (ed.) (1994). *The Condition of Citizenship.* Thousand Oaks, CA: Sage.

Vegh, S. (2003). Classifying forms of online activism: the case of cyberprotests against the World Bank. In Michael D. Ayers & Martha Mccaughey (eds.), *Cyberactivism: Online Activism in Theory and Practice* (pp. 72–3), New York: Routledge, 2003.

Vyzoviti, S. (2001). *Folding Architecture: Spatial, Structural and Organizational Diagrams.* Amsterdam: BIS Publishers.

(2003). *Supersurfaces: Folding as a Method of Generating Forms for Architecture, Products and Fashion.* Amsterdam: BIS Publishers.

Walker Rettberg, J. (2008). *Blogging.* Cambridge: Polity Press.

Walther, J. B. (1995). Relational aspects of computer-mediated communication: experimental observations over time. *Organizational Science*, 6, 186–203.

(1996). Computer-mediated communication: impersonal, interpersonal, and hyperpersonal interaction. *Communication Research*, 23, 3–43.

Walther, J. B., Van Der Heide, B., Kim, S. Y., Westerman, D. & Tom Tong, S. (2008). The role of friends' appearance and behavior on evaluations of individuals on Facebook: are we known by the company we keep? *Human Communication Research*, 34(1), 28–49.

Warren, S. D. & Brandeis, L. D. (1890). The right to privacy. *Harvard Law Review*, 4, 220.

Wasserman, S. & Faust, K. (1994). *Social Network Analysis.* Cambridge: Cambridge University Press.

Webster, F. (2006). *Theories of the Information Society.* London: Routledge.

Weintraub, J. (1997). The theory and politics of the public/private distinction. In J. Weintraub and K. Kumar, *Public and Private in Thought and Practice* (pp. 1–42). Chicago: University of Chicago Press.

Weintraub, J. & Kumar, K. (eds.) (1997). *Public and Private in Thought and Practice.* Chicago: University of Chicago Press.

Wellman, B. & Berkowitz, S. D. (eds.) (1997). *Social Structure: A Network Approach.* Greenwich, CT: JAI Press.

Wellman, B., Haase, A. Q., Witte, J. & Hampton, K. (2001). Does the Internet increase, decrease, or supplement social capital? Social networks, participation, and community commitment. *American Behavioral Scientist*, 45(3), 436–55.

Williams, F. and Pavlik, J. V. (1994). Epilogue. In F. Williams and J. V. Pavlik (eds.), *The People's Right to Know: Media, Democracy, and the Information Highway* (pp. 211–24). Hillsdale, NJ: Lawrence Erlbaum.

Williams, R. (1974). *Television, Technology and Cultural Form*. London: Routledge.

(1983). *Towards 2000*. New York: Pantheon / Random House.

Wolfe, A. (1997). Public and private in theory and practice: some implications of an uncertain boundary. In J. Weintraub and K. Kumar (eds.), *Public and Private in Thought and Practice* (pp. 182–203). Chicago: University of Chicago Press.

Worms, J. P. (2002). Old and new civic and social ties in France. In R. Putnam (ed.), *Democracies in Flux* (pp. 137–88). New York: Oxford University Press.

Wuthnow, R. (2002). Bridging the privileged and the marginalized. In R. Putnam (ed.), *Democracies in Flux* (pp. 59–102). New York: Oxford University Press.

Young, J. R. (2007). An anthropologist explores the culture of video blogging. *Chronicle of Higher Education*, 53(36, May 11) http://chronicle.com/ (accessed July 2007).

Index